Kent Island

Kent Island

THE LAND THAT ONCE WAS EDEN

Janet Freedman

Maryland Historical Society
BALTIMORE

Library of Congress Cataloging-in-Publication Data

Freedman, Janet, 1945–
    Kent Island : the land that once was Eden / by Janet Freedman.
        p. cm.
    Includes bibliographical references.
    ISBN 0-938420-84-4 (alk. paper)
        1. Kent Island (Md.)—History. 2. Kent Island (Md.)—Social life and
    customs. 3. Freedman, Janet, 1945—Childhood and youth. 4. Kent Island
    (Md.)—Biography. I. Title.
    F187.C5 F74 2002
    975.2'34—dc21

                                                          2002070274

Printed in Canada.

The paper used in this publication meets the minimum
requirements of the American National Standard for Information Sciences
Permanence of Paper or Printed Library Materials
ANSI Z39.48-1984.

To my family

especially to the memory of my grandmother

Jeannette Elizabeth Samm Nash

Contents

Acknowledgments

This book was begun as my graduate project in the Johns Hopkins University MLA program. My thanks to the outstanding faculty, and to Dr. Nancy Norris-Kniffin, who directed the program at that time. My research was dependent on the voices of a number of Kent Island "old-timers," including my mother, Margaret Nash Whittle, and aunt, Jeannette Nash Clevenger. My appreciation to them and to the many others who shared their time, their stories, and their photographs with me. Special thanks to the Kent Island Heritage Society for allowing me the use of their collection, and especially to Mrs. Myrtle Bruscup, who manages their library files.

Thanks and love to my family, especially my husband Irving, son Jason, and daughter Jeannette, for their love and support through both my mid-life educational experience and the publication process. Acknowledgment to all who have contributed to the richness of my life, including teachers and friends Jean Rubin, Ann Rasinsky, Gloria Hevia, and Linda Mayberry. Especial thanks to Werner Erhard, who taught me to follow my dreams, to stand and deliver, and to stop whining and get the job done. Love and gratitude to Singy Tevis, who exudes positive energy, cheerleads the dreams of her friends, and who told me with great regularity that I *could* write this and that I *would* have it published. Finally, my thanks to my editor, Donna Shear for her skill, her sensitivity, and her heart.

Janet Freedman
Baltimore

Prologue

The two men walk in front of me through an expanse of open field, their heads bent in easy conversation. We started out this walk together, but I am now a grateful ten paces behind, free to absorb this sun-spangled afternoon unconstrained by conversation. It is a bright and glorious day; the sky a wide and rich enamel blue, the grasses of the field as high as my thighs, the breeze playing and dancing through the meadow, the sun as warm and golden as memory.

These men are a contrast. My friend, Moncure, is a budding and energetic entrepreneur. He walks briskly, his pale hair glinting in the sunshine, intently engaged in conversation. My cousin, Bob, his hair darker and cropped, is the taller and slimmer of the two, and he is, as always, quietly precise and as steady as a boulder. Moncure came with me to the island today. Although we've planned to look about the island and to have a seafood dinner at one of the Kent Narrows restaurants, primarily we are here so that I can show Moncure this land, this farm that was once my grandmother's and is now for sale. Bob, who understands plats and markers, had graciously agreed to meet and walk the land with us. I do not know what he thinks of this; he has not said. Moncure is a developer. He is exploring the possibility of duplicating his outlet mall successes at this site. And why not? In my childhood the seclusion of Kent Island was altered forever with the building of the Chesapeake Bay Bridge and the pouring of that first concrete highway. Bridges and roads quite naturally bring people. Development after development has followed, all greeted as progress, the natural beauty and splendor of the landscape subdued by more houses, marinas, restaurants and stores. When my grandmother, conquered by age, moved from this land to live part of the year with my mother in Baltimore, and part of the year with Aunt Jeannette in Grasonville, I had no further reason to come here. I divorced myself from this farm, from this land I had known with intimacy for all of my life. It has been transformed through no fault or choice of my family from a quiet farm to commercial property; it had ceased to be how it was and my ties to it ended completely with my grandmother's death.

Moncure and Bob have reached the highway that cuts through the farm, their conversation ended in the whoosh and roar of passing cars and trucks. They are waiting for me. But I am having trouble walking on this uneven ground, in this jungle of briar, grass and wildflower, with these tears that suddenly sting my eyes. I tug impatiently at a briar that catches my skirt . . . I am not dressed for this . . . I have forgotten . . . I have the wrong clothes, the wrong shoes. And I am suddenly aware, with a pain that is almost physical, how dear this land is to me.

In the jumble and immediacy of living, I have misplaced the memory of all the endless days of childhood when I ran, joyous and free, in these same wild, fragrant fields. With my grandmother's death and with the growing, unstoppable development of the island, I have, with some intention, forgotten the feel of this place.

"Stop it!" I tell myself angrily as I hastily wipe my eyes with the back of my hand. This is simply a piece of property. It must be dealt with. It is on the market. Either Moncure will buy it or someone else will. Standing along the highway, it is doomed to inevitable development. This farm was all my grandmother had, and it must be sold to settle her estate. There is nothing I can do about it.

I continue walking, searching about me for familiar landmarks. I know that the old house, barn, and outbuildings are gone, but I think I can approximate their location amidst the unrestrained greenery. The landscape has become so overgrown that I am having difficulty recognizing exactly where I am. The lines between field and lawn have long ago been erased. There is a large spreading tree in front of me. I study it questioningly, and then, suddenly, and with a heart-leap of joy, I recognize it. It is the mulberry tree. Planted by my grandfather at the edge of the lawn, it was a fixture and constant of my childhood. I have spent more afternoons than I can count beneath its generous branches. Once it stood on an expanse of grassy lawn, but now it stands before me, its great hulk choked with weeds and saplings, an abandoned friend.

The men have continued walking. They are even farther ahead now. I cannot keep up. I cannot stop the emotions that now storm around me. And I cannot stop the tears. I could not have imagined that this would happen: that the fields around me, the spreading mulberry, the space where the house once stood, would now reach out and unexpectedly grip my heart. It overwhelms me, all this beauty, all this loss . . . all this memory.

The Nash House

The Nash house was a frame house of traditional design, built in two sections; to the east was a one-and-one-half story section dating from the second quarter of the nineteenth century; to the west was a two-story section, the first story of which may have been contemporary with, or slightly later than the east wing, razed in the nineteenth century.

A large brick chimney was within the west end of the east or kitchen wing, with a large fireplace in the kitchen, but closed. An enclosed stairway wound to the attic story north of the chimney. The exposed roof rafters were pit-sawn, joined at the ridge with mortise and tenon. Attic flooring was attached with cut nails.

In the two-story section, each floor contained two rooms of approximately equal size. The west chimney was a single flue for stoves. An enclosed staircase rose in the northeast corner of the easterly room. Doors were vertical boards, beaded, nailed to ledges with wrought iron nails. Some mid-nineteenth-century cast-iron locks remained on doors. The attic floor joists and rafters were circular sawn, the latter mitered at the ridge.

— Mildred C. Schoch
Of History and Houses: A Kent Island Heritage, 1982

The Land that Once Was Eden

From the City to the Shore

When I was a child, the island was Eden. In my mind's eye I can repossess at any moment the tang of salt marsh, the swooping flight of seabirds, the grit in the oyster shell lane; a richly detailed remembrance of places and people much loved and not forgotten.

We would travel from Baltimore in our '48 Chevy, my parents in the front seat, my father driving with one arm on the window ledge, a Lucky Strike dangling from his fingertips, his sheaf of dark hair blown in the wind. In later years, when I first read Fitzgerald at school, my mind flashed up this image of my father, a Great Gatsby turned family man, tooling down Old Maryland Highway 50.

Relegated to the back seat with my torturer-brother, I sat brim-filled with anticipation, my feet atop the blue metal cooler containing our lunch. In addition to luggage, the car was packed with foods gleaned from the diverse markets and bakeries of Baltimore—fat juicy oranges, hands of bananas, rich German buttercakes, and delicate star-shaped cookies topped with chocolate or raspberry jam. The back window abounded with breads: soft rolls and Vienna, pumpernickel, and Italian loaves peeked from their paper envelopes. The cooler held (in addition to lunch) cold cuts, cheeses, thickly sliced bacon and fat sausages securely wrapped in crisp white butcher's paper.

In my youthful perception, the drive was eternal. We drove a labyrinth of streets, passing neat brick houses, corner stores, and row upon row of the marble front steps for which Baltimore is famous. We passed the shabby storefronts and tenements west of Johns Hopkins Hospital where women sat on front stoops, their children scampering on the cracked concrete pavements. The asphalt streets wound through downtown canyons of government buildings and offices of decorous dark stone, past large department stores with luxurious display windows, past markets and wharves that smelled of fish, steel, bananas, and spices.

Slowly disentangling from the clamor and traffic, we crossed

The ferry slip at Sandy Point. (Kent Island Heritage Society)

Baltimore's harbor at the Hanover Street Bridge, leaving behind the foundries and factories, the gray docks and oil-slicked marshes of the city. The little Chevy picked up speed, its wheels click-clicking on the seams of the concrete roadway as we passed through the expanding suburb of Brooklyn, past Ferndale, and onward to Glen Burnie. I watched with pleasure as development slowly gave way to small towns and then to open fields and farmland, the sky growing bigger and bluer and wider. Scenery flew by the window as the car pressed onward past Annapolis, the land growing sandier and steadily flatter, until, at last, we reached the ferry embankment at Sandy Point. Joining the line of cars, we devoured our sandwiches while waiting our turn to enter the clanking cavern of the ferry that would carry us across the Chesapeake. Through choppy dark green waves, the air crisp with salt and mingled with the smell of gasoline, we traveled to the island landing at Matapeake.

The Matapeake Indians

The Matapeake ferry landing was named for the Indian tribe that populated Kent Island before the arrival of the Europeans. Little was recorded about the tribe, and references regarding the Matapeakes are sparse. They were members of the Algonquian nation and, according to several references, they first settled at Indian Spring but then moved to Matapeake Neck (or creek) to avoid encroachment by settlers. A nineteenth-century writer observed: "At an early period, the Matapeaks lived upon Kent Island. Their name is still perpetuated by a small stream. And upon the farm held by the late General Emory is 'The Indian Spring.' There also was a large number of arrowheads, and other relics. And in the same part of the island is a neck of land, which for a long time bore the name of Matapax."[1]

There are numerous mentions of Matapax Neck in the *Isle of Kent Land Records* for 1640 to 1658, and it is generally believed that the present-day Batts Neck and the estate of Goose Hill are the original Matapax Neck. The land records describe the surveying of land there for William Medcalf and Thomas Yewell, two of Captain William Claiborne's men at the 1631 settlement.

7th September 1640
William Medcalf and Thomas Yewell of the Isle of Kent planters pray to have confirmed to them the Neck of on the East Side of the Said Island called Mattax Nech which they now hold by Grant of Capt. William Clayborne . . .

25th September 1640
Laid out for William Medcalf and Thomas Yewell a Neck of Land called Mattapax Neck bounding on the North with a Creek in Piney Bay called Mattapax Creek on the West with a line drawn from the head of a branch in the Said Creek, called Medcalfs branch, Southeast unto a branch of Goose harbour (in the Said Pinie bay) called Cedar branch on the South with the

Published in 1751, Joshua Fry and Peter Jefferson's "map" portrays the shipping of tobacco in early Virginia and Maryland. (Maryland Historical Society)

Said branch & on the East with the Said Goose harbour Containing 130 acres or thereabouts.[2]

In *The Origin and Meaning of the Indian Place Names of Maryland*, Hamill Kenny noted that Matapeake was the historical name of the Indians of Kent Island who lived on Matapax Neck and at Indian Springs.[3] It seems probable that the Matapeakes originally lived on the southeastern side of Kent Island. With the arrival of the settlers, they were gradually pushed northward, perhaps first to Matapex Neck, and ultimately to the Broad Creek location very near the Matapeake ferry landing bearing that name today.

It is likely that the Indians migrated from the more southerly location shortly after Claiborne's colony was established. The Matapeakes, like other aboriginal populations, did not fare well after the white man's arrival. What is known is that their way of life was similar to that of the larger and more well-documented tribes (such as the Nanticokes, Choptanks, and Pokomokes), and that they lived in villages. They were not warlike and subsisted on a combination of fishing, hunting, planting, and gathering. They seemed to have lived in relative peace until the arrival of the white man, with the exception of periodic raids by the physically larger and more bellicose Susquehannocks sweeping down from the north. The Susquehannocks considered most of the land surrounding the bay to be their territory and would periodically move into the area to raid, hunt, and fish. They were described by earlier explorers as giant-sized people well versed in the ways of war, resulting from their territorial disputes with the more vicious Iroquois to the north. Captain John Smith, who seemed to have established a good relationship with the Susquehannocks, gave this description:

> Such great and well-proportioned men are seldom seene, for they seemed like giants to the English . . . their language it may well become their proportions sounding from them as a voice in a vault . . . their attire is of skinnes of beares and wolves . . . one had the head of a wolfe hanging in a chaine for a jewell . . . the calfe (of one warrior) was three quarters of a yard about, and all the rest of his limbs so answerable to that proportion that he seemed the goodliest man we ever beheld.[4]

Seventeenth-century observer George Alsop gave an equally fearsome description when he wrote that they were "a people cast in the mold of a most large and Warlike deportment, the men being for the most part seven foot high in latitude, and in magnitude and bulk suitable to so high a pitch."[5]

Emily Roe Denny suggests that such descriptions might not have been completely exaggerated "for when the foundations for the bridge across the Octoraro Creek in Cecil County were being prepared a number of skeletons of extraordinary size were unearthed."[6]

The lifestyle of all of the Eastern Shore tribes required the use of large tracts of land for hunting, gathering, and crop rotation. This included the setting of intentional fires to aid in entrapping game and in encouraging the establishment of new low growth vegetation, such as berries and wild greens.[7] The encroachment of the settlers on more and more Indian land made normal means of survival and sustenance difficult. Another deterrent to survival was the disease brought by the settlers for which the natives had no defense. Historian Robert J. Brugger concluded that while the native tidewater populations proved resourceful and adaptable, "by 1650 disease had reduced their villages to mere shells."[8] Referring specifically to the Matapeakes, Bernard Steiner stated that "These Indians must have suffered from the white invasion, for although Claiborne in 1631 found about 100 of them, by 1641 they seem to be all disappeared."[9]

Moreover, some settlers could not or would not distinguish between friendly and hostile tribes, and those who were peaceful frequently suffered as a result. Colonists had good reason to fear certain Indians (such as the Susquehannocks and Wiccomesses) but one can expect that there were incidents when the innocent were mistaken for the aggressor. The Matapeakes, therefore, might easily have been harmed by being included in various movements, proclamations, and attacks meant for more hostile tribes. For example, on the 10th of July, 1641, the governor issued the following proclamation:

> Whereas it is necessary at this present to stand upon our guard against the Indians, these are therefore to publish, and strictly to prohibit all persons whatsoever that no man presume to harbour or entertain any Indian whatsoever after notice hereof, upon pain of such punishment as by martial law may be inflicted; and I do hereby authorize and declare it lawful to any inhabitant whatsoever of the Isle of Kent, to shoot, wound, or kill any Indian whatsoever coming upon the said island, until further order be given herein.[10]

Bloody Point, at the southern end of Kent Island, was possibly the site of an Indian massacre carried out by the colonists:

> An atrocious massacre was once perpetrated upon these Indians

The Indians of early Maryland as imagined by a British engraver in 1743.

by the colonists, who invited them to an interview, and while they were performing their humble salutations, slaughtered them without warning. The legend associates this cruel deed with a barren spot, still called "Bloody Point," a little northwest of Kent Point, the southern extremity of the island.[11]

We do not know the names of the tribes referred to in these and other references to hostilities towards natives. We know that other tribes, the Ozinies and Monoponsons, for example, lived on or near the island (Monoponson is the Indian name of Kent Island), and that other tribes visited as well. The situation is further complicated by the aboriginal system of naming that was quite unlike the European standard:

We find innumerable names of divisions of these people, for Algonquins had a way of moving in small groups to new localities and calling themselves by various names, usually those of the streams beside which they made their homes.[12]

The site of a store and post office called Mattapex exists on the lower island, and a property called Mattapax sits on the east side of the road to Kent Point. A farm called Indian Springs (perhaps the location of the original Indian Spring) survives on the island, and Truitt reports that "the present owners . . . have in times past used the spring for watering stock. It is now silted and almost impossible to locate exactly."[13] The creek referred to in several manuscripts and the small stream that Davis mentions are unknown.

J. T. Scharf wrote in his history of Maryland that in 1879 "a remnant of the tribe, about fifteen in number, were still surviving on the island about a hundred years ago."[14] Scharf also provided what is perhaps the last whispered shadow of the Matapeakes when he cited this poignant quotation from a letter written by James Bryan. Bryan, a Revolutionary soldier born about 1755, wrote about his childhood memory in a letter to George Lynn Lachlan Davis:

> I remember the Indians; their last dwelling place was upon the northwest side of the Island near the mouth of Broad Creek; and they lived in their cabins of bark upon a small tract of woodland . . . I was then a well-grown boy. They always seemed friendly. I also remember the time of their departure. They left the island near the mouth of the creek, and turned their faces westward. They were the last of the Indians upon the Island.[15]

The Ferries

The Matapeake ferry was one of several ferries that served Kent Island over time. The first ferry to cross the bay ran from Annapolis to Broad Creek. Reginald Truitt's history of Kent Island observes that it is unclear precisely when this ferry started, but "there is evidence to support the conclusion that the line was established as part of a north-south route in the mid-1660's."[16] The first Eastern Shore ordinary (public house or inn) was located at the Broad Creek ferry location as early as 1668, and it was also the location of the first church, courthouse, and jail. Broad Creek was an important stopping place for those traveling to Philadelphia and New York. The following advertisement from the *Maryland Gazette* is dated December 31, 1767:

> This is to acquaint the public that the Subscriber has procured himself good boats and hands to cross the Bay from Broad Creek to Annapolis, and from Annapolis to Broad Creek on Kent Island, and will carry passengers as follows: Man and horse at 10s.; single man, 5s.; single horse 7s. 6d; chair 7s. 6d. He likewise keeps a house of entertainment at Broad Creek on Kent Island, where travellers may depend on being used in the kindest manner by
> JOHN BRYAN[17]

Correspondence to Governor Horatio Sharpe discussing the establishment of post offices is dated at the court of St. James on October 19, 1763; it also refers to what was by then an established "ferry house":

> A rout from Annapolis in Maryland to the several Parts of that Province where it might be proper to settle Post-Offices. From Annapolis (where a Post Office is already kept) across the Bay of Chesapeak to the Ferry House on Kent Island (12 miles). From the Ferry House on Kent Island to Queen's Town in Queen Ann County.[18]

We know that Broad Creek was still in use as late as 1858 as evinced by an advertisement in Centreville's *State Right's Advocate* by a William Goldsborough. The ad offered to the public "a comfortable two-horse stage to and from Centreville every Monday and Wednesday, and from Centreville to Broad Creek every Tuesday and Thursday. Fare from Centreville to Annapolis, $2."[19]

At a later date, ferries traveled from the Light Street piers in Baltimore to Love Point at the northernmost tip of the island. Passengers could continue their journeys by making railway connections at Love Point for trips farther east, or even as far as the Atlantic beaches. The iron-hulled, double-ended ferry *Philadelphia*, known fondly as "*Smokey Joe*," made the two-hour-forty-minute roundtrip three times daily. She was a great icebreaker in winter, defying the odds to cross and re-cross

My aunt, Jeannette Nash Clevenger, posed beside a Claiborne-Annapolis Ferry Truck in 1935. The truck door reads: "Visit the beautiful Eastern Shore via the Claiborne-Annapolis Ferry. Saves 100 miles." (Author's photo)

the bay. Despite her clumsy appearance and masculine name, *Smokey Joe* was a heroine for many, as she completed numerous rescues while going about her daily route. She once liberated an icebreaker that had become hopelessly trapped in the ice, and she regularly rescued other victims of accidents, boat fires, disabled vessels, and high seas. Once she came to the aid of the *City of Baltimore*, a liner bound for Europe that had collided off Seven Foot Knoll with the oil tanker *Beacon*, rescuing the passengers and transporting them to Baltimore.[20] With her large stacks belching smoke and her bulk covered in "a coat of

Smokey Joe *approaches the Love Point pier, 1935. (Author's photo)*

paint red enough to enrage a sea cow,"[21] *Smokey Joe* is the stuff of legends, and her name is still fondly repeated by many old-timers on the island.

The Claiborne-Annapolis Ferry (chartered March 1914, charter annulled February 1934) and the Claiborne-Annapolis Ferry Company (chartered August 1927, corporation dissolved 1941) had boats that traveled from Annapolis to Matapeake. The assets of the Claiborne-Annapolis Ferry Company were taken over by the State Roads Commission of Maryland by an act of the legislature in 1941, and the ferry became the Sandy Point–Matapeake Ferry, operated by the state but doomed by the ongoing plans for the construction of a bridge over the bay.

The Chesapeake Bay Bridge dedication took place on a bright and sunny July day with a lavish ceremony attended by 10,000 people and which lasted several hours. "During those same hours," wrote Brugger, "the Sandy Point–Matapeake ferries, named for governors Nice and O'Conor, sadly made their last voyages."[22]

The engineering report for the construction of the Chesapeake Bay Bridge states that the ferry service had a capacity of "approximately

Passenger cars await embarkation at Matapeake. (Kent Island Heritage Society)

180 vehicles per hour in each direction."[23] The bridge opened to traffic on July 30, 1952, and from that date and the end of the year, bridge traffic totaled 433,851 vehicles. Traffic grew to two million in the first full year of operation (1953) and has steadily increased each year. Statistics for 1998 show that a staggering 23.1 million vehicles crossed the bay on the present double span and officials say they expect a continued increase of approximately six percent per year.[24]

The landing site at Matapeake included a clubhouse with shaded picnic tables along a ridge facing the bay. Many locals have fond memories of weekend gatherings at the Matapeake beach. The clubhouse was used as a meeting place for local organizations and also contained a restaurant. The *Kent Island Bay Times* reported that the State of Maryland turned over the clubhouse, fishing pier, and surrounding land to the Queen Anne's County Department of Recreation and Parks, along with a grant of $85,000 towards renovation of the clubhouse exterior.[25]

The *Governor Harry W. Nice* approaches the pier. (Kent Island Heritage Society)

Our drive from Matapeake to Chester, heading briefly north, then east, was only a few miles' travel. The drive took us past tilled fields and open pasture, where driveways of sand and shell meandered to farmhouses set far back off the road. We passed dense stands of pine, small clusters of houses, a church, a general store, a white clapboard restaurant with the word "EAT" flashing in red neon from its roof. I knew every turn, every landmark; a visual litany of landscape that honed my childish anticipation.

My grandmother's house sat on a low rise, its narrow lane of sand and oyster shell curving gently past the barn, ending abruptly in the front yard. It was surrounded by a wide green lawn, several outbuildings, and a riotous abundance of trees and shrubs. The interminable trip at last at an end, I burst from the car like a racehorse from the gate, rushing to the waiting arms of my grandmother. I knew, and had always known, that though I was perfect nowhere else, for this woman I was entirely so. She was perfect for me as well, as was this place. Beyond the cool shade of her porch, draped in the white light of a blinding summer sun, the farm, the woods, the marsh, and creek shore beckoned in shimmering splendor.

Parents, being practical creatures, somehow remained curiously untouched by the magic in their surroundings, insisting that the car be unloaded immediately. I was assigned the smaller bags and packages and was soon trekking from the car to the house with my little bundles. No matter. I would have made a room-by-room pilgrimage anyway, delighting in the familiar, assuring myself that there had been no drastic changes in my absence. The house was like a favored, multi-patterned quilt, each detail known, yet every nuance a newfound delight. I knew the look of it, the feel of it, the sounds and smells of it; it belonged as much to me as it had ever belonged to anyone.

The house was of frame construction and built linearly in three sections, the first being a deep porch entered by a screened side door. The porch itself was solidly walled to hip height and screened upward to the eaves. Because it boasted an almost constant breeze and a pleasant view, it served as both parlor and dining room for most of the year, abandoned only when winter's chill finally drove us indoors.

The floor was covered in several linoleum patterns, the predominant one of dark blue scattered with gaudy peach cabbage roses. In the center of the house wall, a door led to the kitchen and was flanked on one side by a large white icebox and a wringer washer draped in oilcloth, on the other by a medicine cabinet, a mirror, and a porcelain sink set in a wooden frame.

In the center of the room was a claw-footed dining table (for which my grandmother seemed to possess an endless supply of extension leaves), and lining the walls were various benches and oaken chairs to be drawn up to the table at mealtime.

And what meals that table held! The generosity of sea, orchard, and garden arrived at that oilcloth covered expanse, each one in its season . . . platters of fish and eel; briny oysters; crabcakes, abundant with lump backfin, spicy and fried golden brown; fat ripe tomatoes

My grandmother and I pose in the garden, 1946. (Author's photo)

fragrantly warm from the garden, steaming ears of sweet corn; paper-thin cucumber slices in a tangy onion-studded vinaigrette; peas with dumplings; biscuits and blackberry rolls; strawberry cakes and lemon meringue pies. I remember as well the table covered in layers of newspaper and piled high with steaming blue crabs, turned bright orange from the cooking, crusted with pepper and fragrant with spices, the best of the Chesapeake's feasts.

The kitchen was bright and cheerful with wainscoting and chair-rail, and a table and chairs enameled a rich Dutch blue. A built-in corner cupboard lined with flowered shelf paper displayed dishes and platters of varying color and design, including many in the blue willow pattern. It was a sunny room owing to two large windows, and it was equipped with a large wood stove, a gas range, a small refrigerator, a sink with a hand-pump, a treadle sewing machine, and several freestanding cupboards. A small closet tucked under the attic stairs held pots and pans and a wooden caddy crafted by my grandfather for the storage of silverware.

When I was very young, a favorite kitchen activity was watching the train go by. Hearing its whistle in the distance, I would scramble for the window, standing on a chair to watch it pass . . . black and mighty, belching smoke . . . the Maryland/Delaware/Virginia branch of the Pennsylvania system, once the Queen Anne's railway,[26] dashing across the wide amber fields.

In the northwest corner of the kitchen, two steps led to a door of vertical boards that opened onto narrow curving stairs reaching to an attic room above. Sunshine streaming through the bubbly glass windowpanes and the chimney rising from the kitchen below kept this small space warm and dry, thus deemed by my grandmother a perfect place for the storage of onions and potatoes, hung in bags and bunches from the rafters. There was little else; a few oil lamps saved for possible power losses, some nails, a ball of sisal twine, harvested seeds waiting to be planted. The bareness was a disappointment to my sense of exploration. The barn loft, when last I looked, had been equally bare. Where were the items my mother spoke of: a spinning wheel, a butter churn, my great-grandfather's law books? I questioned my grandmother.

"Burned," she said.

"Why?" I gasped.

"They weren't being used," she tartly replied.

Recipes Served on the Porch

CUCUMBER SALAD

2 medium cucumbers
salt and pepper to taste
small chopped onion
3 strips of bacon, chopped (may substitute fatty ham)
vinegar (1 to 3 ratio with bacon fat)
pinch sugar (if desired)

This recipe is simple to prepare, although it takes several hours. Cucumbers, particularly their skins, were considered to be "poisonous," thus cucumbers were pared before salad preparation. Slice the pared cucumbers into paper-thin rounds, salt, and let sit at room temperature for several hours. (This process removes additional "poison.") The salting process will draw moisture from the cucumbers. Squeeze them to remove as much of the liquid as possible, discard the liquid and place the cucumbers in a serving bowl. Add chopped onion. In a skillet, fry the chopped bacon until crisp, add vinegar, pepper, and sugar (if desired) and pour the mixture over the cucumbers. Serve at room temperature. This recipe can also be prepared with torn garden lettuce or leftover cooked green beans.

POOR MAN'S CAKE

1 lb. brown sugar   2 cups water
2 tbsp. shortening   3 cups flour
1 box raisins   1 tsp. baking soda dissolved in
1 tsp. cinnamon   1 tbsp. hot water
1 tsp. allspice

Mix together the first six ingredients and bring to a boil, cooking for 5 minutes. Cool. Stir in the flour and baking soda mixture. Pour into a tube cake pan. Bake at 350 degrees for approximately 1 hour.

BREAKFAST FISH WITH BACON

8 cleaned white or yellow perch
12 strips of bacon

Choose a pan that is wide enough to hold the fish comfortably and deep enough that they can be immersed in water during cooking. Fill the pan with water and bring to a simmer. Put fish in the hot water and simmer until just done. While the fish is cooking, chop the bacon roughly and sauté until crisp. Remove fish from liquid and place it on a platter. Pour the bacon and bacon fat over the top.

FRIED EELS

2 eels
salt
lard

Eels are delicious and easier to eat than fish because they have only one bone. But live eels can give you a nasty bite. The best way to avoid this is to knock them senseless before you begin by hitting their heads against a wall or step. Cut the head *almost* entirely from the body, then pull the head in a downward motion, using it as a "handle" to peel the skin from the eel. Cut the eel from end to end along its underside, removing intestines and scraping with a sharp knife along the backbone. Cut the eels into 2 to 2½-inch pieces, salt liberally and refrigerate, covered overnight. When ready to prepare, rinse eels under cold water, again scraping along the backbone to remove any blood. Melt lard in a skillet until hot, add eels and cook until browned and tender.

ROLLY-BOLLY

4 medium apples (or an equivalent amount of peaches or berries)
1 ½ cups sugar
1 pint water

For the Dough:

2 cups flour	2 tbsp. sugar
4 tsp. baking powder	3 tbsp. shortening
½ tsp. salt	½ cup milk or water

Put sugar and water in a baking pan and warm over a slow fire. Sift dry ingredients together; cut in shortening and liquid to make soft dough. Roll on floured board, approximately ½ inch thick, spread with fruit, sprinkle with sugar and cinnamon to taste, and dot with butter. Roll up, tucking in the ends and place in the warm syrup, seam side down. Sprinkle with a dusting of additional sugar. Bake in a hot oven until fruit is done and dough is browned.

My mother, Margaret Nash Whittle, poses in her high school graduation gown. She was a member of the twelve-student Class of 1931. She made the outfit, beginning with the undergarments, in Home Economics class. It was a requirement for all female graduates. (Author's photo)

PEAS AND DUMPLINGS, ETC.

1 cup flour	1 tbsp. lard
1 tsp. baking powder	water (1/3 cup or more)
¼ tsp. salt	

Mix dry ingredients. Add enough water to make a soft dough. Roll on floured board as thinly as possible. Cut into small or large squares as desired. Drop into boiling water, soup stock or soup. Stir to keep dumplings from lumping together. Boil for just a few minutes until done.

These dumplings can be mixed with cooked green peas or lima beans just before serving. They can also be added to stews and soups, and are particularly good with chicken.

STEVENSVILLE HIGH SCHOOL BISCUITS

My grandmother, like many older cooks, did not have a written recipe for her breads and biscuits. The following recipe is similar to hers, and was the one taught to my mother in cooking class at Stevensville High School in 1928:

2 cups flour	4 tsp. baking powder
½ tsp. salt	2 tbsp. fat (lard)
approx. 2/3 cup milk or water	

Mix dry ingredients. Work in fat with fingertips or cut in thoroughly with a knife. Mix the liquid with the dry ingredients. The mixture is the right consistency when it is "spongy." Roll gently into ½-inch thickness on a lightly floured board and cut into biscuits. Place on a baking sheet and bake in hot oven.

The largest and more recent section of the house, built in the mid-nineteenth century, was two storied, with a parlor and bedroom downstairs, and two bedrooms above. In the southeast corner of the parlor, a duplicate of the paneled attic door opened to reveal the narrow staircase that wound upward to the bedrooms.

The parlor had a large kerosene stove. It and the kitchen were the only heated rooms in the house. In winter, my grandmother lit the kerosene stove in the small dark hours of the morning. She had already started the kindling in the kitchen wood stove as well, and it snapped and crackled with burning logs and pinecones. I was briefly and gloriously thankful for their warmth when I descended from the icy upstairs bedrooms but would soon make my escape to the yard, my coat unbuttoned, the cold of winter a relief.

The parlor was furnished with a cut velvet couch, various fat and overstuffed chairs, a high-backed rocker, and a Seth Thomas pendulum clock, obtained through the saving of coupons. An ornate curio cabinet that had belonged to a great-grandmother stood in one corner, its shelves replete with antique china and small items of the sort that people bring to grandmothers from their various excursions and holidays: tiny little cups and saucers, decorated plates and animals emblazoned with "Blue Ridge Parkway," "Ocean City, Maryland," and "New York World's Fair."

There were several windows in the parlor and two exterior doors, one opening east into a shrubbery garden, the other opening west into the shade and feathery foliage of a Japanese walnut tree. In the heat of summer this was a favorite afternoon reading spot. One could lie on the floor in front of a screened door, bathed in a cross breeze, the linoleum cool against sunburned skin.

The upstairs bedrooms were equipped with an assortment of furniture: iron beds with long bolster pillows, chests of drawers, chairs, nightstands, chiffonniers, a washstand with a flowered bowl and pitcher, and an ornate pier mirror which my Aunt Jeannette, in her adolescence, painted a shocking mauve and green. The walls were covered with flowered wallpapers, linoleum was laid over the painted plank flooring, and colorful rag rugs were scattered about the floor.

"We used to have wool rugs when I was young," my mother told me.

The Nash house viewed from the shade of the mulberry tree, 1940. (Author's photo)

"What happened to them?"

"Oh, they were so much work. Your grandmother would take those rugs up every spring and carry them to the yard to beat them clean. Then they would be carried back up the stairs and tacked down with black carpet tacks."

I was certain that my grandmother did not miss those rugs. Only my toes lamented their passing when they touched down on the shocking cold of January linoleum. In the winters of my childhood, clad in floor-length flannel, I would snuggle down on icy pillows and be covered with an almost unmovable weight of blankets and patchwork quilts. Clothes for the next day would be laid out by my bed. Rarely, in the chill of morning, would I have the courage to dress here, but would dash downstairs to change by the warmth of the wood stove.

In the summer I would sleep with my head at the foot of the bed to be close to the window that opened into the upper branches of the walnut tree. On still summer nights I was grateful for each small breeze that moved through the fern-like foliage, joining the frogs and crickets in their evening serenades.

25

The Kent Island Colony

Kent Island was settled in 1631 by William Claiborne. A stockholder in the Virginia Company and official surveyor of the Jamestown colony, Claiborne saw the possibilities for establishing his fortune in the New World. An educated and enterprising man, he earned an excellent reputation in Virginia, becoming a member of the Governor's Council and subsequently appointed secretary of state. In 1627 he sought and received permission from Virginia's governor to explore the Chesapeake Bay and establish trading arrangements with the Indians. It is likely that on his first exploratory trip Claiborne decided on Kent Island as his main wilderness outpost.

> The Susquehannocks had their villages on the lower Susquehanna River, on the border between Maryland and Pennsylvania, and they claimed dominion over Maryland territory as far south as the Patuxent on the western shore of the bay and the Choptank on the eastern. Claiborne purchased Kent Island from the king of the Susquehannocks for [a] trunk valued at twelve pounds sterling.[27]

We assume as well that Claiborne chose to name his newly acquired property the "Isle of Kent" in remembrance of his home in Kent, England. The island was a natural choice. Located approximately halfway between the Jamestown colony and the mouth of the Susquehanna River, it was well situated for trade. Claiborne sought to establish a fur trade with the Susquehannocks, as their lands ranged northward where superior furs could be obtained. The island was home to the unwarlike Matapeakes, offered a defendable site, good harborage, and fertile land for cultivation.

A return trip to England secured Claiborne the financial backing of Clobbery and Company, a well-established merchant firm anxious to profit from the lucrative fur trade. Clobbery provided funds to establish the outpost, promised Claiborne a percentage of the profits, and gave him full authority in managing the Chesapeake enterprise. With

An undeveloped creek and marsh. Much of the island must have looked this way when Claiborne arrived. (Author's photo)

an initial group of one hundred men, Claiborne established a colony near the southern tip of the island, built a fort, and parceled out land. The colonists established friendly relations with the Indians, the island had plentiful timber, and the fields and forests were abundant with nuts, berries, game, and wildfowl. The bay, rivers, and creeks supplied many varieties of fish as well as oysters, crab, and clams. The colonists built gristmills and homes, established gardens and orchards and, within the first year, were represented in the Virginia legislature.

At the same time that Claiborne was founding his colony, George Calvert, the first Lord Baltimore, was petitioning King Charles I of England for a second land grant in the New World. With an earlier grant he had founded the colony of Avalon in Newfoundland, but the severe climate and rocky soil—and his own declining health—combined for an unsuccessful outcome. Calvert, a fervent Roman Catholic, dreamed of establishing a colony where his faith could be practiced with freedom and without fear. He had visited Jamestown (where he was viewed with suspicion as an interloper) and knew that the milder climate, fertile soil, and abundant wildlife of the Chesapeake region would provide many of the attributes missing in Avalon. His illness overtook him, however, and he died before his court intrigues against opposing agents of the Virginia colony had delivered his longed-for grant. In June of 1632 King Charles I signed the charter establishing Lord Baltimore's colony, naming it Terra Maria in honor of his queen, Henrietta Maria. The grant encompassed an area north of the Potomac described as lands "uncultivated and unplanted and inhabited by barbarous tribes of Indians" and included Kent Island. It fell to Calvert's son Cecil, the second Lord Baltimore, to deliver on his father's dream and establish the colony of Maryland.

Claiborne, who by that time was well established on the island, protested and disputed Lord Baltimore's claim. His position was that the grant, by its very wording, excluded Kent Island because the land contained in the grant was specifically described as "uncultivated and unplanted," which was certainly not the case at Kent Island. Claiborne's claim was staunchly supported by the Council of Virginia, who felt that the Kent Island settlement was by now an established part of the Virginia colony. Then Leonard Calvert, the brother of Cecil, was named governor of the Maryland colony and accompanied the settlers bound for the Chesapeake. He must have known that a resolute enemy awaited him.

After much skirmishing between Claiborne's Virginia outpost and the new Maryland colony (including the first naval engagement in North American waters), Governor Leonard Calvert subdued Claiborne's followers by force. In the midst of the turmoil, Clobbery and Company withdrew their support (some say at the behest of Lord Baltimore). Additionally, the Lord Commissioners of Trade in London ultimately decided that the title to Kent Island belonged absolutely to Lord Baltimore.

The *Ark* and the *Dove* brought Calvert's settlers to what became St. Mary's City in 1634 to establish the first settlement under the land grant. While it was the first settlement by Calvert, it was clearly not the first settlement in Maryland. That distinction belongs to the defiant William Claiborne and his colony at Kent Island.

The exact location of Claiborne's settlement has never been firmly established. We do know that his personal plantation was called Crayford or Crayford Fort, though none of the structures existing on that property today are any earlier than late eighteenth-century. In speaking of the gristmills, Truitt reported in 1981 that "two stones from them recently have been discovered at Crafford,"[28] a farm located near the Kentmor development. These appear to be the only surviving physical remnants of Claiborne's colony. Like the Matapeakes, dust in the wind.

Love Point

Legend tells of a beautiful Indian maiden who fell in love with a handsome young Englishman, perhaps even one of Captain Claiborne's own crew. A warrior of a neighboring tribe had earlier sought the hand of this beautiful maiden and was angry that she had chosen another. One night the jealous warrior attacked and killed the young Englishman, and the young woman, inconsolable, died of a broken heart.[29] The point of land where this tragedy is said to have taken place was thereafter named Love Point in memory of the young couple who lost their lives for love.

While one might scoff at this legend of love, there is no argument that both Love Point and the resort that bore its name were beloved by locals and crowds of happy vacationers for many years. Love Point is located at the northern tip of Kent Island, where the resort sat on a bluff overlooking the spot where the Chester River flows into the Chesapeake Bay. During the heyday of steamboat travel, sidewheelers such as the *Dreamland,* the *Westmoreland,* and the *Emma Giles* brought throngs of vacationers to the pier, a massive wharf one hundred feet wide and

The sidewheeler Westmoreland *steams out of Baltimore. (MdHS)*

Women, possibly hotel staff, walk near the Love Point Hotel. (Kent Island Heritage Society)

projecting 1,250 feet into the Chester River. It is easy to imagine those Edwardian ladies, their long organza dresses swishing at their ankles, escorted from the boat by gentlemen wearing stiff straw boaters and starched collars.

On a nearby hill sat the Love Point Hotel with its broad veranda, excellent dining room, bath houses, and picnic groves. There was a beautiful sand beach and a lake for canoeing. Additional amenities included a bowling alley, shooting gallery, dance pavilion, and a board-walk of amusements, including a merry-go-round. Local watermen could be hired to take out fishing parties. Other vacationers tried their luck at crabbing from the pier.

Day-trippers came to picnic under the trees or to enjoy a sumptuous dinner from a hotel menu featuring fresh local fish, crabcakes, soft-shell crabs, fried chicken, and shore-raised corn, tomatoes, peaches, and strawberries. Other visitors came to spend a week or more, taking up residence in the high-ceiling rooms, relaxing in rocking chairs on

Love Point -- The Resort

Although Love Point has for several years been considered the most ideal spot on the Chesapeake Bay as a picnic and bathing ground, it was not until two years ago that the plan was concieved of converting it into a summer resort. The plan was readily adopted, in view of the fact that very few changes were necessary, the greatest advantage of natural beauty and location being supplied by a generous Nature. Last year a beautiful hotel, with all modern improvements of electric lights, water and baths, was erected, and later, owing to the rush of guest, it became necessary to enlarge the building. This was done, and a magnificent hotel now stands there.

Advertisement for Love Point Resort. From Where River and Bay Waves Meet.

the wide porch after a day of activities and waiting for the dinner bell to ring. Years before the advent of air-conditioning, Love Point offered cool bay breezes and respite from the heat of the city combined with entertainment and relaxation.

It is difficult to determine the exact year that the hotel was built, and published dates have ranged from 1890 to 1913. The original structure was built by Hugh Pope and contained ten bedrooms and a large dining room and kitchen. Within a short time he sold the hotel to the Love Point Beach and Park Company of Centreville. A brochure entitled *Where River and Bay Waves Meet* was distributed by that developer and is undated. The popularity of steamboat travel helped make the resort a successful venture, and a second building was soon added to accommodate the flood of guests arriving from the city. The addition was three stories high with thirty-nine rooms.

Phil Kemp, a grandson of two of the principals in the Beach and Park Company, reported that in his childhood he would watch as many as three steamboats pull up to the pier on a Sunday afternoon. "They'd all be loaded with passengers" he said, "and we figured on getting about one-third for supper." L. L. Hubbard, who leased the hotel in the mid-1920s, said that Love Point Hotel was also known as a honeymoon

Hallway sign from the Love Point Hotel. (Kent Island Heritage Society)

hotel and was so popular with Maryland politicians that it was dubbed "The Little White House." Advertised as "Maryland's Grand Old Hotel" the resort also hosted events such as the 1908 clay pigeon shooting championship attended by the legendary Annie Oakley.[30]

Encouraged by success and optimistic for the future, the Love Point Beach and Park Company began planning an extended resort community for the site. They laid out an entire town with a network of streets and avenues and offered 350 building lots for sale to the public at prices ranging from $100 to $600.

Despite the hotel's popularity, plans for expansion never materialized. The company apparently had financial difficulties, and although they rebounded several times, there were mortgage defaults in 1916, 1917, and 1923.[31] Despite the failure of the company's expansion plans,the hotel remained popular. In the ensuing years, it was overseen by a number of managers and leasing agents, and despite significant changes the hotel remained profitable. But as steamboats replaced sail on the Chesapeake Bay, ferries gradually replaced steamboats for transporting Love Point's clientele. An advertisement from the 1930s pro-

Advertisement for building lots at Love Point Beach.

motes Love Point as a "Family Hotel on the Chesapeake," quoting a
weekly rate of eighteen dollars, but only eight dollars per week for
parents with children.[32] That same flyer lists a steamboat and ferry
schedule of six roundtrips per day between Baltimore and Love Point.
The Pennsylvania Railroad maintained a ferry service from Baltimore
connecting at Love Point. The train stopped at many shore towns, finally terminating its run at Lewes, Delaware. There were two ferry

Advertisement for building sites "Where Breezes Blow All Summer."

boats—the *Pennsylvania* and the *Philadelphia*—the famous *Smokey Joe*.

Before I was born—before my parents owned a car—they would travel from the Light Street pier in Baltimore to Kent Island aboard *Smokey Joe*. Though the Love Point Hotel's heyday was past, it continued in operation, and vacationers would stay the night or dine at the hotel before boarding their train for the Atlantic beaches. Locals also frequented the hotel, and Saturday night dances and Sunday dinners remained popular. While still in operation, there were several unsuccessful attempts to revive the hotel's past glory. But transportation was increasingly limited. The railroad ceased passenger service in 1938, and the ferry schedule was cut and finally halted completely in 1947. The hotel was subsequently closed. Like similar resorts conceived in the heyday of steamboat travel, the demise of the Love Point Hotel followed the gradual reduction of boat traffic, and it was ultimately passed by for the growing boom of the Atlantic beach communities. Finally, the Pennsylvania Railroad leased the pier to a salvage company.

In 1964, the hotel and grounds were sold to C. J. Langenfelder and Sons of Baltimore. They acquired the pier and converted a smaller building to office space, but the hotel was too large for their use. It sat abandoned on the hill, gradually falling into disrepair, and was occasionally the target of vandals. On the afternoon of November 12, 1965, the Queen Anne's County Fire Board in Centreville received several calls reporting that the hotel at Love Point was on fire. The aged wooden structure burned rapidly. Within twenty minutes the building began to collapse, and "in thirty minutes nothing was left but a pile of smoldering rubble and two chimneys outlined starkly against the skyline." The police gave the verdict of arson, though the culprit(s) were never identified. The *Kent Island Bay Times* commented that the old hotel's last customer was a firebug.[33]

Today, C. J. Langenfelder & Sons continues dredging operations from the Love Point site. As outlined in an agreement with the State of Maryland, a portion of the dredged shell is used to build up new oyster beds at locations stipulated by the state; another portion is ground and marketed by Langenfelder for a variety of uses, such as roadway base.[34] The hard, grating sounds of the dredge and the shell pulverizing equipment dominate Love Point today. One can still make out the railroad

The Love Point Hotel completely engulfed in flames. (Kent Island Heritage Society)

turnaround in a swath of green grass to the right of the road. Nothing remains of the Love Point Hotel.

On May 26, 1917, in the midst of the steamboat era, the *Baltimore Sun* published the following poem by Folger McKinsey, who became known as the Bentztown Bard:

LOVE POINT

To Love Point with Dearie, to Love Point away,
The light in the Chester, the isle in the bay;
To Love Point with Dearie, and baby and all,
The boat's at the pier and the heart hears the call.
To Love Point with Dearie
A luncheon for two;
The *Westmoreland* blows
And the broad bay is blue!

To Love Point with Dearie and Lord bless the child
Whose lips are of rose and whose heart's beating wild!
Haul in the gang plank and cast off the line
To Love Point with baby and Dearie for mine!
To Love Point the beauteous
To Love Point the calm,
The sweet Isle of Kent
And the blue bay of balm!

To Love Point with Dearie, fried chicken and cake
And catsup and pickles — what else need we take?
To Love Point the airy, that headland so dear
Where all the blue dream of the broad bay is near!
To Love Point the airy,
The fairy, the sweet,
With joy over head
And green grass under feet!
To Love Point with Dearie, up early and off,
The tugs in the Basin are beginning to cough;

The great ships are turning, oh watch them and fly
Afar with the dreams to the blue Kent-land sky!

To Love Point, the joyous.
Sweet Eden of earth.
With baby and Dearie,
And hearts full of mirth!
To Love Point with Dearie, sweet cookies and tarts.
Dear dreams of long days in the dreamland of hearts;
Away with the morning to fly on the wing
Of the ships of the Basin to fair lands of spring!
To Love Point and Chester,
The light off the bar
And home o'er the foam
'Neath the moon and the star!

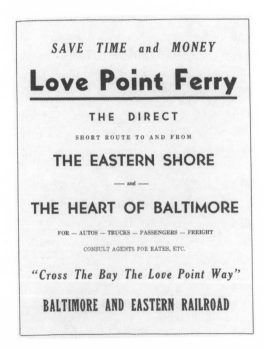

Advertisement for the Love Point Ferry. (Kent Island Heritage Society)

I would wake to the sound of birds. In the city I saw an abundance of English sparrows and blackbirds, but there were a great variety of birds on Kent Island: the little bobwhite that called from the fields, evening whippoorwills, squawking blue jays, catbirds, swallows, and red-winged black birds. Baltimore orioles built a hanging nest in the cherry tree, and grandmother's "little jenny wren" returned each year to the tiny birdhouse attached to the milk house wall.

Above my bed the portraits of my grandmother and grandfather looked out over the room. Engagement photographs, posed in a Baltimore studio, they have curved bowed surfaces and ornate gilt frames. My grandmother wore a long bustled dress and a plumed velvet hat, her elbow resting on a marble pedestal, a potted palm in the background.

"Oh, how I hated that hat!" my mother once told me.

"Why would you hate it?" I asked, surprised at the fervor in her voice. "I think it is a pretty hat."

"Well, it wasn't pretty to me. . . . I almost died of embarrassment over that hat! We had to walk to the Chester school and if it was raining, your grandmother would make me wear that hat because we didn't have an umbrella. Guess we couldn't afford one! We were poor but didn't know we were poor because everybody else was nearly the same way. But I hated the hat; everybody laughed at me.

"Oh," I said, remembering my own embarrassments, my stomach knotting in sympathy as I imagine her walking off to school.

"Was that her wedding dress?" I ask, wanting to change the subject.

"No, her wedding dress was white organdy, very simple. She cut it up one Christmas to make doll clothes for Aunt Jeannette and me. It was a pretty dress."

And a true gift, I think, to have cut up her wedding dress for two little girls.

My grandfather's photograph is of a dapper young man, looking southern aristocratic in his Ashley Wilkes attire and small, smart moustache. Later photographs have shown him broader and balder, his moustache larger and pure white. I lament never having known him,

Engagement photographs of Jeannette Elizabeth Samm and Robert Ephriam Nash, 1904

as he died four years before my birth. But I have heard the stories and they are full of spit and fire, gentleness and generous humanity, and I have loved every one. I am told that we would have been great friends.

It was hard to imagine that these people in the gilt frames were relatives of mine, and that the elegant young lady in the plumed hat was now likely sipping her coffee on the downstairs porch. She would have finished her breakfast and chores, and would greet me with a "Good morning, sleepyhead" even though it was barely 8 A.M.

Kent Island Grammar Schools

A booklet published by the Kent Island Heritage Society lists eight white schools and three Negro schools operating on the island within living memory, many of them in nineteenth-century buildings that saw use well into the twentieth century. Its table of contents lists the schools:

Upland Island School or Middle District School or
     Skinner's Gate School
Chester Negro School
Stevensville Schools
Batt's Neck Negro School
Middle District (between Kent Point & Stevensville)
Up Island Negro School
Kent Point School
Coxes Neck School
Chester Elementary School
Dominion School
Love Point School

The Chester School attended by the Nash children was the second structure to house that elementary school. The first building had been located several miles from the farm.

The first school in Chester was known as Sharktown. It was situ-

Postcard featuring Chester School and Piney Creek. (Kent Island Heritage Society)

ated off Route 552. A road known as the Old Tom Price Lane, next to the first Tom Price Store, led back to the little schoolhouse. This was on the farm property owned by the Ringgold family. It was a one room school similar to the other schools on the island and was built around the middle nineteenth century. John O. Phillips was the first teacher in 1858. His salary was $100.00 per year.[35]

The Chester School, to which my mother walked in her embarrassing hat, was the second and "new" school building. It was built around 1900 on Route 18 between Benton's Store and the Lee Bell property, approximately one mile from the Nash farm. It was originally constructed with two rooms, one in front, the other in back, though another room, a hallway, and entrance were added to the front of the building as enrollment grew.

"There were two classrooms in front, the new room had the first, second, third grade, and part of the fourth. The original front room was larger and the rest of the fourth grade was there along with the fifth, sixth, seventh. Each room had a coal stove that sat on a metal base in the middle of the room. I think that a man living nearby took care of them. We're lucky we didn't burn up, 'cause in the summertime they used to oil those floors to keep down the dust."

"And we didn't have running water, either."

"No, Lordy. Mr. Lee Bell was next to the school. He was the station agent and was one of the trustees or something. We would go over to Bell's and get a bucket of water and sit it in the hallway and everybody drank out of that same dipper."

"And we didn't die of disease either!"

Disease, however, did visit the school on occasion as demonstrated by the documented appeal of a teacher named Mr. DeLauder who went to the school board in 1906 requesting full pay for a period during which the school was closed due to a diphtheria epidemic.[36]

In the 1920s the Dominion School transferred the fifth, sixth, and seventh grade classes to Chester Elementary. In 1927, Dominion School closed completely and the remaining students also came to the Chester School.

"Oh, I remember those ornery boys from Devil's Dominion! We said to our selves, 'Oh my they are coming in here and messing us up!' But a lot of the boys didn't stay in school too long. They had to work on the farm or they went to the water."

"But some of them would hang around the school sometimes. Once we were selling chances on a cake and one of them older boys said, 'No, but I'll take a chance on you!' That was forward talk in those days. I went right home and told it."

To help raise funds, the students sometimes sold magazine subscriptions and the school sponsored suppers and cake raffles. The Chester School was closed in 1956. Improved roads and transportation allowed transferring the children to a newly built elementary school in

William Nash prepares to walk to school, ca. 1915. He carries his book pouch over his shoulder and his lunch in a lard bucket. (Author's photo)

The Nash cousins and siblings stand in front of the milkhouse. Front: Jeannette Elizabeth Nash, Arthur Steward (Bud) Nash. Second row: Myrtle Irene (Babe) Nash, Margaret Ethel Nash. Third row: Charlotte Louise (Lottie) Nash. Back row: Arthur Orville Nash.

44

Stevensville, designed to absorb the enrollment of the scattered small schools and serve the entire island. The Chester School building was subsequently used as doctor's offices. At a later date, local businessman Billy Harris[37] converted the building into four apartments. It was recently deliberately burned down to make way for the construction of a Rite-Aid pharmacy and parking lot.

My Mother's Coat

When my grandparents' first child arrived, he was the first boy to be born in the family in awhile. When he was old enough to go to school his Aunt Kate, who lived in Baltimore, sent him a little white fur coat. Over time it was passed on to the next child and then the next, and finally to my mother.

"It was the custom in those days to allow the seventh-grade children the privilege of bringing a little friend to school for a day's visit if they would be entering first grade the next year. My friend Amy Tolson, who lived just across our field, got Mom's permission to bring me along to Chester School. I was very excited and anxious to walk to school with the older girls and sit on the big bench in the schoolroom. I can't remember how the day was spent but I do remember that I liked it very much . . . so much that I was willing to stand up at closing time and address the class. I wanted to tell them about the wonderful coat that Amy was helping me with."

" 'See this coat!' I said proudly. 'First it was Ed's . . . then it was Robert's . . . then it was Willie's . . . then it was Orville's . . . and now it's mine! Next I guess it will be Jeannette's!' "

"Was Mom embarrassed as this tale was related to her? You can bet she was. But she was the one to pass it on. So I think she enjoyed it too."

Mom Mom Nash in 1968, at age 89. (Author's photo)

My grandmother was most often found on the porch. She wore buttoned-front cotton dresses with lace-edged lapels in tiny prints of miniature bouquets or strewn rosebuds. She said that when she was young her hair was thick and long enough to sit upon, but in my memory it is cut, softly gray and neatly permed under her hairnet. Her once smooth checks were patterned with the lines and wrinkles of age, hard work, and Chesapeake sun, but her eyes were still young and sparkling with humor.

We called her "Mom Mom." I thought it a silly and embarrassingly frivolous name. I once tried unsuccessfully to enroll my brother and cousins into calling her the more dignified "Grandma" (or better yet, the "Grandmama" I found in Victorian novels), but since I was one of the youngest of her grandchildren, the name was firmly established and unyielding to my opinion.

My grandmother was born in Baltimore in 1879, the daughter of German immigrants. Named Johanetta Lizbeth Samm, she used the Anglicized Jeannette Elizabeth, but was simply "Miz Nash" or "Miz Nettie" to her neighbors and friends.

My grandmother and I had always been related, not simply by blood. Alone with her often when I spent long summers at the farm, we would sit on the porch in the heat of midday and at twilight through dark, sometimes speaking, sometimes quiet in comfortable affection. I am like her in my joy of stove and cooking and in my propensity for digging in sweet, deep earth. I cherished her. A woman of grit, unpretentious yet having great dignity, stubborn at times, persistently willful in the face of age and arthritis, tender and gentle, she sat serene and peaceful on her porch.

Breakfast on the wide-screened porch offered fried eggs, sliced tomatoes, toast, and a variety of my grandmother's fruity homemade jams. There was often bacon or sausage, and, if anyone had been successful fishing the night before, we would have a banquet of fish, poached and topped with crumbly bacon.

My father and brother, sated with breakfast, would wander off to the creek as my mother would begin to clear away the breakfast dishes. She would put a kettle on the stove to heat the water needed for the soapy dishpan.

I would be sent to retrieve the bottle of rubbing alcohol from the cabinet tucked under the parlor stairs. Mom Mom would patiently dab the alcohol on the red itchy mosquito bites I had acquired during the night.

"They sure do like you!"

"Why do they bite me so much? They haven't bitten you."

"That is because I am old and stringy. My skin is too tough for them. But you are sweet and tender."

I never thought that the alcohol did much to relieve the mosquito bites but I would submit to the ritual. I likely did more damage to my skin in one day than the mosquitoes would ever aspire to. I was always barefoot and barelegged in summer, a fearless adventurer, empress of all I surveyed, my kingdom waiting just outside the green screened door.

There was never a question of what to do but of what to do first. The yard was full of offerings. The little ornate milk house and the well; beyond them the ancient pear trees, the strawberry patch, the meat house, and the spreading mulberry hung with swings. Past the trees were the fields, then the pinewoods, silent and scented, stretching down to the salty creek. To the right of the lane was a two-storied barn and a cowshed sheltered by towering black walnut trees, a vegetable garden, the outhouse hidden in dark red climbing roses and set among beds of flashing orange tiger lilies. There were mounds of lilac and snowball. In the spring their petals fell like snowdrifts on the newly green grass.

Next came the fruit trees, not large ones like the ancient pears, but smaller and planted in neat rows: plums, cherries, white and yellow peaches, Hard Red and Pippin apples, tiny Seckel pears and an arbor of dusky blue Concord grapes.

The shrubbery in the side yard, probably spaced nicely when originally planted, were as fat and round as matrons in hoop-skirts. I would squeeze past their branches to watch the hummingbirds and to discover nooks yet uncharted, places to remember if my cousin Janeen suggested a game of hide-and-seek.

My cousin, Janeen Clevenger Jewell (right)—now the owner of Crown Jewell Travel in Chester—and I admiring the flowering snowball bush in our grandmother's garden, 1947. (Author's photo)

Something was always blooming there. There were azaleas, forsythia, flowering almond and weigela; roses of talisman, deep red, pink, and pure white; fat peonies of mauve and white with their heads heavy with dew, and several hydrangeas of varying shades of blue and lavender. There were beds of august lilies, sweet william, chrysanthemums and zinnias; little rows of purple and yellow-faced pansies and tubs of riotous Mexican roses flashing magenta, yellow, and orange. My grandmother liked to plant things. My grandfather had been a gardener as well. Someone has been planting in this sweet earth for several hundred years.

Kent Island Economy

Though the island's seventeenth-century economy began with Indian trade, Claiborne's colonists were soon tilling the soil of Kent Island. Indeed, one of the attractions the island held for Claiborne was the fertility of the land. Claiborne's other trading outpost, at Palmer's Island, was rocky and not suitable for planting. Claiborne had wisely realized that in addition to producing food for their own consumption, he and the settlers would have to produce crops that could be traded for the English commodities needed in their New World settlement. Beaver pelts, however valuable, were not collected in quantities sufficient to fill a ship's hold, thus other products must also be available to tempt English trading vessels to travel the additional miles up the Chesapeake. As a solution the colonists cut lumber from the forests and, like their Virginia neighbors, grew tobacco and corn for shipment to England.

Calvert's ultimate victory over Claiborne in the land grant dispute brought further colonization of the island. As more settlers arrived additional crops were planted. Rent rolls for the period indicate that settlers frequently paid fees in supplies of tobacco, corn, or other commodities selected "at the choice of his lordship."[38]

From the colony's earliest years, planters grew tobacco. Tobacco eventually became so widespread as a cash crop that the proprietary government offered inducements to farmers to encourage the sowing of grains, and ultimately passed laws to penalize farmers for the exclusive sowing of tobacco.

> An Act of 1649 provided that every taxable person planting to-
> bacco should also plant and tend two acres of corn on forfeiture
> of 50 lbs. of tobacco for every half acre he should fall short of the
> proportion, besides 50 lbs. of tobacco per acre to be paid to the
> constable and his assistant.[39]

One method for purchasing tobacco involved small boats sitting at anchor, waiting to receive tobacco; this practice was seen later in nine-teenth- and twentieth-century oyster "buy-boats" that would wait for the oystermen's catch. One of many examples of such trade appeared in the *Queen Anne's Court Records:*

MARYLAND
Queen Anne's County

This is to certifie whome it doth or may concern that John Dunkin, commander if the Ship *Chester River*, now Rideing at anchor in Chester River, in the aforesaid province and from thence bound for London, in Great Britain, will take Tobaccos on board the said ship on Freight at the rate of seven pounds, sterling money of Great Britain, per Ton. Given under my hand the 14th day of April, Anno Domini 1726.

Jno. Dunkin[40]

In an Act of 1763 the government began regulating the inspection of tobacco and allocated six public warehouses to Queen Anne's County, placing one of them at Kent Island. During the American Revolution, however, planters were cut off from their British markets, and out of necessity farmers began to plant other crops, especially corn and wheat. After the war's end, tobacco farming declined, as farmers had established new markets for cereal grains. Tobacco had proven to be a soil-exhaust-ing crop, requiring farmers to abandon fields or plant them with less demanding crops after several seasons. In 1794 several warehouses were discontinued and in 1807 three others, including the one at Kent Island, were sold.

> By the middle of the eighteenth century, Kent Island, which had been so strongly contested in the seventeenth century, settled down to a more or less uneventful existence. The period of the beaver trade was already a remote memory, and the middle of the eighteenth century marked the end of tobacco cultivation on Kent Island.[41]

The tobacco cultivation of the eighteenth century took its toll on the region. Without crop rotation and fertilizers, farming methods were inadequate and further eroded soil quality already depleted by tobacco. Crop yield was reduced. Other, non-agricultural developments contributed to the area's decline. The successful completion of a new ferry line from Annapolis to Rock Hall soon diminished Kent Island's Broad Creek as an important point on the Virginia to Philadelphia route. Not only did the Rock Hall line deposit travelers farther north, but the double embarkations and disembarkations required at Kent Island likely contributed to the demise of the Broad Creek ferry line. At any rate, Kent Island decreased in agricultural and economic importance, receding from the significant position it had occupied in both the seventeenth and eighteenth centuries. The island became a backwater, and a haven for watermen and farmers.

Many men who worked the water also maintained gardens to supply the produce needs of their families, and larger farmers sent crops by sloop and ferry to Western Shore markets. Kent Island's recovering sandy loam became a source of fruits and vegetables for the growing populations and canneries of Baltimore. Dr. Julius T. Ducatel, examining the Eastern Shore soils centuries after the demise of tobacco remarked that:

> In Piney Neck, situated between Back Wye and the Eastern Bay, the soil is mostly a clayey loam. Such likewise is the nature of the soil in the greater portion of Kent Island, fitted by proper management and perhaps destined by the advantages of its situation

> *I started crabbing as a boy, taught by my grandfather. If I had put a sponge in the barrel, my grandfather would have kicked my butt. I was 15 years old when I started tonging and crabbing. Got my first boat when I was thirteen.*
>
> Billy Harris

to become at least the subsidiary of Baltimore County, for the supply of the growing wants of the great mart of the State; it should be covered with vegetable gardens and orchards.[42]

Agriculture continued to be of prime importance on the island, with varying crops of wheat, corn, soybeans, melons, tomatoes, and berries accompanied by orcharding, poultry production, and the raising of dairy and grazing herds. It is certain that the visitors to the Love Point Hotel dined on locally grown products.

From the beginning, of course, Kent Islanders harvested the abundance of the Chesapeake's waters. Many families earned their entire income—or supplemented farming income—with the seasonal harvests of fish, crab, and oysters. The business of working the land and working the water was handed down from father to son.

Johanetta Lizbeth Samm and Robert Ephriam Nash were married in Baltimore on March 9, 1904.

"Pop," known to everyone on the island as "Captain Eph," was an oysterman and a farmer and along with his father, operated what we believe was the first oyster packing house on Kent Island, at Bryan's Cove. He later moved the operation to Kent Narrows, operating under the name "Nash Brothers," moving crates of iced oysters by rail to Love Point and then by steamer to the Port of Baltimore.

"Who was the other brother?"

We are on the porch. Mom Mom is seated in her usual straight-backed chair, her hands moving quickly as she crocheted a lacy lavender edging on a crisp cotton handkerchief.

"His younger brother, Arthur. Pop promised his mother on her deathbed that he'd see to it that Arthur was taken care of, so he took him into the business as a partner."

"Didn't go too well, though," she continued. "Arthur wasn't a businessman, and it was hard having the business support two families."

She sighed. "After Pop died, I sold Arthur my half, probably for a lot less than I should have, but I was worrying over it all the time, afraid he might lose it and then I wouldn't have anything. But Arthur didn't live too many more years himself. Bad heart. Just like Pop."

In entering the oyster trade, grandfather had followed in the footsteps of his father, Charles Maltimore Nash, a partner in the firm of Armiger and Nash, Oyster Commission Merchants, with offices in Baltimore at the corner of Cheapside and Pratt. Their firm had been one of the fatalities of the Great Fire, which burned more than 150 acres of Baltimore on February 7, 1904.

"And the truth will never be known about that one," she said, hinting at something darker beyond the facts I knew.

"What do you mean?"

"Oh, it just looked like there was some robbery done then. Everybody thought so."

"Robbery? Tell me!"

"Well, their offices burned all right. Practically the whole downtown burned. It was a terrible sight to see, all the smoke, the fire jumping from building to building. I saw it for myself."

"What were you doing there?"

"I lived there. Your grandfather and I weren't married yet. I still lived with my family in South Baltimore, over near Fort Avenue. My sisters and I watched that fire from up on the roof of our house."

"Wasn't it dangerous?"

"No, the fire never got anywhere near the south part of the city. What with the harbor cutting in right there and the firemen and bucket lines, we could see we were safe."

"So, now what did you mean when you said the truth would never be known?"

"Well, your great-grandfather was here on the island. He ran the business from this end, mainly. Mr. Armiger said that everything was gone. Everything. And all the records lost. No record of all the money owed to them."

"And it wasn't true?"

"Well, nobody rightly knew. It just seemed funny, that's all. Mr. Armiger seemed to make out all right, in fact, more than all right after the fire. A lot of people said he had saved more than he let on, took stuff out of there before the fire got the place . . . the records and all, and he went about collecting the money later. Kept it all for himself."

"And my great-grandfather didn't do anything?"

"Couldn't. Couldn't prove anything. Especially from way down here. Lost a lot then, excepting the Beach Farm."

I am both amazed and indignant at such treachery. "They didn't do anything?" I ask again incredulously.

"Oh, Pop wanted to go up there and set things right. But he was young and he had a hot temper. I think his father was afraid of what he might do. At any rate, he was against it and Pop didn't go."

It is easy to see that this incident was a turning point in the family fortune, a downward turn from which we apparently never recovered. I hated to think of those Armigers who probably live fat and happy in Baltimore while my grandmother was so poor. They should have done something, found out the truth, fought back, rather than losing so much.

Chesapeake Oysters

William Claiborne and his men traveled to Kent Island from Virginia, and there may have eaten their first Chesapeake oysters. If not, they would likely have been introduced to the bivalves by the Matapeake or Monoponson tribes once the settlement on Kent Island had been established. Although an excellent source of protein, the oyster was long considered a poor man's food until benefiting from a growth in popularity that began in the 1700s and continued through the 1800s and beyond. As a result, oysters became a thriving industry in Maryland and an economic mainstay and way of life for many inhabitants of Kent Island. As historian John Wennersten noted, "Oysters, once hardship's food, grew in popularity. By 1779 advertisements for oyster sellers in Maryland, New York and Massachusetts were widely circulated from Boston to Williamsburg."[43]

As early as 1811, New Englanders who had overharvested their local beds by dredging, began moving into the Chesapeake region to harvest oysters. The oysters were sold or were transplanted into the depleted beds of Long Island Sound. Northern dredge boats were not welcomed by local watermen, who regarded the "arsters" as their own. Both Maryland and Virginia moved to protect their economic interests. "Virginia in 1811 passed a law forbidding dredging within her waters. Maryland went further in 1820, restricted oyster catching to ordinary tongs, and forbade transportation out of state in vessels not owned by her citizens.[44]

New England businessmen such as Caleb Maltby, Daniel Holt, and Abiathar Field moved to Baltimore and became leaders in the expanding oyster-packing industry. While their primary motive might have been avoidance of the aforementioned transportation law, it is more likely that they saw the great opportunity in new markets created by the construction of the Baltimore & Ohio Railroad. While early oyster packers sent freshly shucked oysters in ice by wagon over the Cumberland Road, the building of the railroad opened markets from Pittsburgh through the Ohio River Valley and into the Midwest. This trade was in fresh iced oysters and "cove oysters,"[45] a spiced or pickled version that had a longer shelf life due to heavy doses of vinegar. The development of commercial canning or the "hermetically sealing" process in Baltimore made the city a leader in the canning industry and made possible the shipment of oysters almost anywhere. While pickled and canned oysters found audiences in more distant communities, fresh oysters enjoyed an increasing popularity and growing demand in larger cities from the East Coast into the Midwest:

> In the 19th century, the American people were enveloped in a "great oyster craze." No evening of pleasure was complete with-

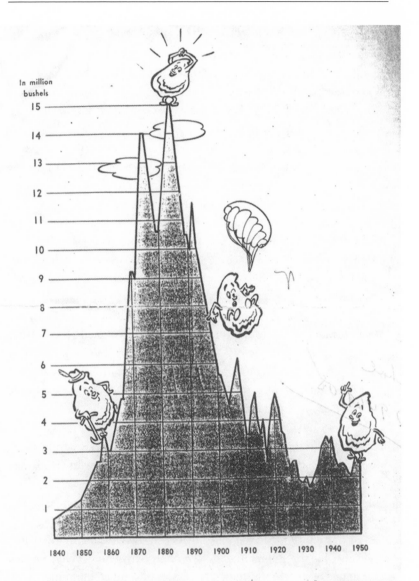

The ups and downs of oyster production

Source: Official State Publications

43

"Maryland's Sunken Treasure." (Courtesy Maryland State Department of Education, 1953)

My, on the first day of oystering, I have seen one hundred boats on the bar of the Chester River! It was beautiful—skipjacks, schooners, bugeyes, pongees—It was quite a sight. We got twenty-five to thirty cents a bushel for oysters then, and the catch was fifty to one-hundred bushels a day.

— Billy Harris

out oysters, no host worthy of the name failed to serve "the luscious bivalves," as they were actually called, to his guests. In every town there were oyster parlors, oyster cellars, oyster saloons, and oyster bars, houses, stalls and lunchrooms.[46]

The Chesapeake oyster harvest continued to grow, reaching its peak in 1885. Even with later reductions in harvests and the demise of the Baltimore canning industry, yields and sales of fresh oysters were large enough to support significant business on Kent Island. The growth of the local shucking houses at Kent Narrows bears testament to that expanding commerce. While harvest numbers have continued to decrease, oystering continued to support a considerable number of Kent Island waterman:

This carried over until early in this century when local bivalves, greatly depleted, still supported a waterman and labor force of thirteen hundred and some ten or more processing plants on or near the Island. . . . Chester, Dominion, and Stevensville truly are towns built by crabs, fish and oysters—mainly oysters.[47]

The Chesapeake Bay Bridge

They are going to build a bridge across the Bay.

"They won't be able to do it. A bridge of that length has never been built."

"Do they know how deep that Bay is?"

"What about the currents? We all know how strong they are. It will never happen."

"Them fancy engineers will get a surprise! They will never even get the footers done."

"And what about the freighters going into Baltimore? A bridge would just be in the way. You'll have freighters missing the channel and ramming into the bridge."

I was amazed that such a thing could even be imagined. From the island I could not see the Western Shore at all, just the wide and seemingly endless expanse of olive-green water.

Some people were excited about the bridge. They talked of going to the Western Shore for jobs in Annapolis and Baltimore. They said that they would have better places to shop and would no longer have to make the drive to Easton or Denton. They said that the bridge would be good for the local economy, that they would be able to sell seafood and crops at better prices.

My mother leaned over the bed, packing neatly folded clothes into the old brown suitcase.

"As soon as the bridge is finished, we won't have to wait in those long lines at the ferry anymore," she said. *"We will just zip across the bridge."*

I am not sure if this is a good idea. If I can zip across the bridge, then so can a lot of other people. Will this be good?

My grandparents bought their farm in 1919. They had previously lived in a house no more than a mile away and the entrance to my great-grandfather's farm—the Beach Farm—was just at the end of the

My grandparents Jeannette and Ephriam Nash with daughters Jeannette and Margaret at the Beach Farm, 1924. (Author's photo)

lane. The Beach Farm sat far off the road, down a long sandy lane, on the banks of the Chester River.

In my childhood, the Beach Farm was owned by Charles and Leon Crane of Baltimore. They put up a big sign announcing that the farm's new name was "Chesterhaven Beach." The sign also offered lots for sale and outlined the butchering of the farm into housing tracts.

"It will bring a lot of traffic down this road."

"It is too much development for one piece of land."

In their voices I hear sadness and regret.

I am angry with my family for not still owning that farm, for thinking that nothing would change, for assuming that there would always be time. I am angry with the developers. I feel robbed, cheated, my history lost and irretrievable.

I am like the Matapeakes.

"If I were rich," I rage to myself, "I would buy that farm back and I wouldn't care how much they charged."

But I am impotent in the face of my youth and the riches of strangers. We sit on the twilight porch.

"Mom Mom, why didn't you ever live at the Beach Farm?"

"Perhaps I should have," she answered. *"Your grandfather wanted us to move there after his father died, but I didn't want to go."*

She is silent, remembering. I wait for her to go on.

"The farm seemed so far away then, the lane so long, and no other houses nearby. I was home alone all day and the children were babies and only a wagon to get anywhere. I was afraid to be so far. Your grandfather had to sell it, though he didn't want to. I guess it is really all my fault."

I imagine a young woman with tiny babies, alone on that riverfront farm. I imagine an emergency, a horse to hitch to a wagon, the long drive. *"Mom Mom, how did you and Pop meet?"*

Her eyes go away as she remembers.

"I came here on a vacation with my best friend, Lizzie Vogelman. We worked together in a factory in Baltimore. My mother let me join her on a holiday to visit her family."

"And you met my grandfather here?"

"Yes, at the Beach Farm. Your grandfather was her brother."

"Was it 'love at first sight'?"

"Yes," she answers, *"I suppose it was."*

"They had a big wooden outdoor dance floor," she continued. *"And I loved to waltz. I danced with your grandfather that night until I had holes in my slippers."*

"Did you go back to Baltimore?"

"Yes, of course I did. But we wrote to each other."

She smiles in the dark, remembering.

"Then what happened?"

"Winter came. It was a particularly cold winter. I did not receive an answer to my last letter. I waited for weeks. I was very angry and thought he had found someone else. I was never going to speak to him again."

She laughed.

"Yes, yes . . . and then what happened?"

"The mail arrived one day and there was a pile of letters for me. The

bay had been frozen and the mail boat couldn't get through. He had written every day asking why I hadn't answered his last letter!"

I remember the holly tree my mother showed me in the Beach Farm woods. If you walk down Piney Creek Road toward the shore, approximately fifty feet from the farm lane and perhaps fifteen feet from the road, you will find a large, towering holly tree. In its bark are the initials J. S. and E. N. encircled by a heart—Jeannette Samm and Ephriam Nash—carved there long, long years ago by young lovers.

The Nash Family and the Oyster Business

One account records the story of Charles Nash.

> Charles M. Nash was reared and educated in Baltimore and when twelve years of age began learning the ship caulking business under his father. He became foreman in the establishment of William Numsun, oyster packer, with whom he remained for twenty-two years, from 1854 to 1875, at which time he began business for himself as a member of the firm of Armiger and Nash, oyster commission merchants, their place of business being at the corner of what is now Cheapside and Pratt. Mr. Nash has four oyster boats which land at the Pratt street dock and is doing a very successful business. He has a fine country residence and farm on Kent Island in Queen Anne's County, but spends his winters in Baltimore.[48]

The Bryan's Cove oyster house was opened around 1890, and it is likely that it was an outgrowth of the already successful business partnership established with Armiger in Baltimore. It is also likely that my great-grandfather's selection of Kent Island was a natural one as he had historical connections (and probably family) in Queen Anne's County prior to the purchase of his Kent Island residence and the establish-

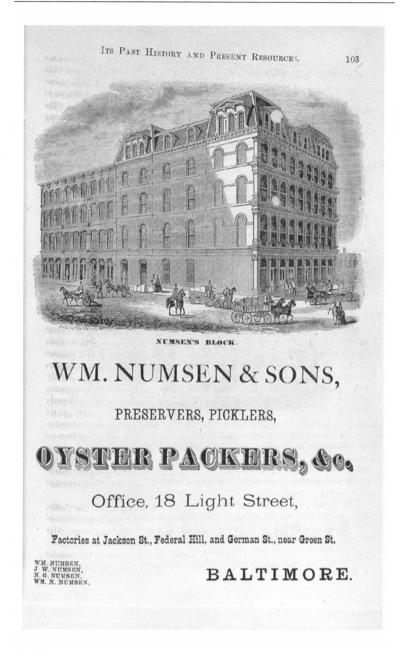

The Wm. Numsen Oyster Packing Company where my great-grandfather learned the oyster business. Reprinted from A. J. Nichol, The Oyster Packing Industry of Baltimore *(University of Maryland at Baltimore, 1937).*

Train crossing Kent Narrows Bridge in 1922. (Photograph by T. Milton Oler Jr. Kent Island Heritage Society)

ment of the oyster house. Thomas Nash, his great-grandfather, was both "a farmer and participant in the Revolution" who "closed his career in Queen Anne's County."[49] His mother, Elizabeth Ann (Young) Nash was the daughter of a Queen Anne's County planter.

The boats mentioned in the above quotation were buy-boats that operated completely under sail and traveled to Kent Island to purchase local oysters. (My mother remembers them beached and rotting on a sandbar near the Beach Farm, relics of the business destroyed in the Baltimore Fire.) The citation also lists Charles M. Nash's children Elizabeth (Vogelman); Catherine (Turner); James A., a Baltimore fireman; William H., an oysterman; Robert E. (my grandfather), "a farmer and merchant on Kent Island"; and the younger John H. and Arthur.

While still a single man, my grandfather took over the operation of the oyster house, later moving it off the island to Kent Narrows. The Narrows, so populated today, was then just an expanse of wetlands. The only oyster house existing at the Narrows at that time was owned and run by Pete Baxter. Their houses sat at the marshy edge of the water on the mainland side. Over the years a number of packing houses sprouted on this stretch of marsh just north of the Kent Narrows Bridge, named after their owners: Holton Harris, Bennie Austen, Johnnie Coursey, Jake Tolson.

> Shucking houses were designed for the survival of the oyster, not the worker. The oyster houses were built at the water's edge so that oysters could be easily unloaded and stored. Yet this proximity to the water meant a damp, if not wet, working environment.[50]

Captain Arthur Jones, who worked at the Narrows as a boy, remembers the area before the marsh was filled in and the oyster houses sat at the edge of the water.

> We would shovel shells all summer. They was as high as a telephone pole. Before they cemented Route #18 they used those oyster shells to fill in that road. We had to lay down boards as walkways over the marsh; it was the only way to get from one place to another.

Ice was chopped from the Chester River or collected from the spring breakup of freshwater ice from the Susquehanna and buried underground, keeping well into the season. The oysters, packed in ice and straw purchased from a local farmer, traveled on the same railway that brought the summer vacationers from the Atlantic beaches to Love Point. The Queen Anne's Railroad stopped at Kent Narrows to take on these shipments of oysters bound for the steamer to Baltimore.

Some oyster shuckers were local but many came down from Baltimore to work during the season. A few brought families, though most were single men, and they lived in the accommodations supplied by management—rows of small two-room wooden shanties located steps from the shucking house.

Mostly the Baltimore shuckers knew each other or were related. I remember my father going to Baltimore to look for them when the season was coming on. If he found one, he pretty much had found them all because they would pass the word that there was work down on the island.

It probably sounds like Pop was the big business man, but it wasn't that way; he was struggling to make a living and take care of his family, just like everybody. He worked long, hard hours. I remember him coming home late, Mom saving supper for him and him having walked the railroad tracks from Kent Narrows to home, his moustaches covered in ice.

And he was known for treating his shuckers fairly—he lent them money, he invited them to the house at Christmas, and when he died, they paid him the tribute of walking from the Narrows to our house. They stood as a group at the edge of the yard, some of them crying. Leroy, he was the foreman in the oyster house, he left and never came back. He said, "I lost the bestest friend I ever had."

They have built a larger road across the island.

It starts where the new bridge crosses the bay and stretches to Kent Narrows, connecting with the small bridge that links us to the mainland. They have taken a portion of my grandmother's farm to build this road, paying her what they say the land is worth. They dug soil from the large field near the woods and used it to raise the new roadbed. It is an open wound, a man-made gully that will grow nothing but weeds.

Yesterday, without warning, they came with their concrete trucks and poured a section of the road. We are penned in and cannot leave our lane until the concrete dries.

They have cut off access to the old graveyard. It sits isolated now beyond a sea of newly poured concrete. I wonder what will happen to those graves?

The State of Maryland and the engineers do not care about such things. They are building this bridge and road to "open up" the Eastern Shore; they are building a shorter route to the Atlantic beaches. We are in the way.

Orville Nash, seated, is surrounded by (clockwise) Edward, Robert, and William Nash. (Author's photo)

Johanetta Lizbeth Nash survived eight pregnancies and bore six children, all born at home with the help of Aunt Georgianna Mealy, an island midwife who was a descendent of slaves. They are, by age:

Charles Henry Edward, born January 30, 1905
Robert Ephriam Jr., born April 25, 1906
William Ernest, born November 8, 1908
Arthur Orville, born October 5, 1910
Margaret Ethel, born September 7, 1914
Jeannette Elizabeth, born June 1, 1918

There is a gilded framed photograph of the uncles in the upstairs bedroom, the older boys surrounding a tow-headed Orville, seated in a chair. Uncle Ed is the oldest and my grand-mother's favorite, even though this fact is vehemently denied. When she was a single girl in Baltimore, a gypsy fortune-teller told her that she would get married, move across water, and would lose her firstborn. Since she did get married and move across water, she has been worrying about the last part ever since.

Uncle Ed went to the city as a young man, where he married and

Grandmother (center) poses with her children on Mother's Day, 1947. They are (l–r) Edward, William, Margaret, Jeannette, Orville, and Robert. (Author's photo)

raised a family. He has since retired back to the island, built a home down the road, grows a small garden and putters about the creek. He is blustery in his opinions, perhaps thoughtless, but meaning no harm. He has a certain innocence; he is, I think, a dreamer. Perhaps this is why my grandmother favors him so.

The Circumstances of Women

Life for most women in the late nineteenth and early twentieth centuries was certainly not one of leisure. Many items of convenience that are a normal part of our lives today had not yet been invented. Some conveniences that were available in the cities were not yet available to country women, and country living brings with it its own set of accountabilities. The chores and daily activities of a Kent Island farm woman in the early twentieth century closely resembled those of a pioneer.

My grandparents, Ephriam and Jeannette Nash, with Phoebe, about 1920.
(Author's photo)

My grandmother's workload was in no way unusual and because my grandfather was a businessman, she may have had it slightly easier than most. From her verbal accounts, I list the following:

Homes were heated with wood and cooking was done on wood stoves. Women routinely chopped and carried wood and gathered sticks and pinecones for kindling. Water came from backyard wells and had to be drawn and carried for all consumption and cleaning needs. A typical wash day would involve rising before dawn to build a fire in the wood stove, drawing water from the well to heat in large pots on the stove before any washing could be accomplished. Clothing was soaked in water and soap, boiled in a large washboiler, scrubbed on a washboard, rinsed with additional water and hung on outside lines. Imagine the volume of work involved in a family of eight! Imagine this in the cold of January and the heat of August!

"I remember those long-johns that Pop and the boys wore. They would come in from the line so stiff from the cold that they could stand up by themselves. Mom would bring them in and put them behind the stove until they were warm and dry enough to wear."

Mom Mom and her Rhode Island Reds, 1942. (Author's photo)

There was no indoor plumbing. An outhouse could be found some-where in the yard. Bathing was accomplished with the same hauling and heating of water that was required for laundry.

Cooking was done on the same wood stove that provided winter heat. Women became accomplished at baking breads, biscuits, and cakes in the small attached ovens heated by wood. My grandmother cooked for a family of eight (again, not unusual). Imagine the work involved in preparing the simplest of meals! Imagine cleaning up af-terwards! Most of the foodstuffs eaten by island families were pro-duced on the farm. Women helped to plant and care for gardens, vines, and fruit trees. They canned and processed the majority of the fruits and vegetables their families ate through the year—not just canned peaches, beans, and tomatoes, but jams, jellies, pickles, rel-ishes, and sauerkraut. Mason jars were used, of course, but heavy containers such as empty King Syrup cans were also used for canning and sealed with heavy layers of wax.

Bins inside the house stored potatoes and onions for winter use. Most families had chicken houses, frequently in the care of the house-

wife. While men often cared for the larger animals, it was not un-
heard of for women to be milking cows and slopping pigs. Pine needles
were often gathered as bedding for hens and livestock.

*"Mom was right proud of her Rhode Island Reds. Pop grew field corn
for the other livestock and she would have the boys crack it up for those
hens. Sometimes we would have to hammer the edges of oyster shells
and scatter it in the yard so they'd have a source of lime. And many the
times I had a cold fried egg sandwich in my school lunch! Ate so many
of them as a kid. . . . that's why I don't like 'em much today!"*

Although women were infrequently involved in slaughtering, they
participated in the processing, salting, and "laying down" of cured
meats. Fish (usually white or yellow perch) were salted down in crocks
for later use.

Cleaning was done without the benefit of vacuum cleaners and
other devices (there was no electricity) or the many cleaning products
available to us today. Sewing was done by hand or on a treadle sewing
machine. Women frequently produced clothing for their families. Worn
items and scraps were recycled into quilts and braided "rag rugs."
Most of this work was done in the evening by the light of an oil lamp.

Cooking, cleaning, and sewing took place alongside the myriad
duties involved in the care and raising of children. Most babies were
delivered at home by midwives with all the accompanying risk. My
grandmother lost her sister-in-law and best friend when she and her
baby died in childbirth.

My uncles have produced a substantial number of cousins who are
scattered about the island and mainland; some live in Baltimore just
like me. All of them are older than I am, some of them married with
children of their own. The exception is my Aunt Jeannette and her
husband William who have produced my cousin Janeen, a compan-
ion of a more appropriate age, and her baby sister, Kathy. They live in

Grasonville, a small town on the mainland, several miles from the Kent Narrows Bridge.

In summer Janeen and I must lobby the adults for transportation—me begging to go to Grasonville, Janeen trying to get to the farm. Janeen manages to persuade with remarkable success, and has succeeded today as well. We have been playing with our dolls on the cool linoleum floor of the parlor. The women are out on the porch, talking quietly, hoping for a breeze. It is very hot.

"Not a breath of air stirring," says Mom Mom.

"Still as can be," says my mother.

"It's the same over in Grasonville," adds Aunt Jeannette.

Mom Mom sits in her straight-backed chair, a fly swatter in her hand. Flies are not tolerated in this house. If one dares to sneak onto her porch, she is ruthlessly single-minded regarding its death.

"Yep, it sure is hot," she says with a sigh.

Janeen and I agree about the heat. We also agree that the best possible thing to be doing on a day like this is swimming. I asked my mother earlier today about going swimming, but she said "no" firmly and I know there is no point in asking again. She will give me *that look,* a message without words that says I have gone too far and to continue would bring consequences. I've never asked what that might be—the look is enough to stop me.

I explain this to Janeen. She ignores me and meanders onto the porch.

"Mom, will you take us swimming?"

"Not now, Janeen."

"But, Mom, it's hot," she protests. "Can't we go swimming?"

"Not now, Janeen."

Well, she tried. They never want to take us swimming anyway. I begin to talk about other games we could play, but Janeen will not be persuaded to consider any of my ideas. Hardly five minutes pass before she is back on the porch.

"Mom, will you take us swimming?"

"Not now, Janeen."

"But Mom, it's hot. Why can't we go swimming?"

"Because you can't, Janeen," replies Aunt Jeannette.

Well, that's that. It was a gallant try. She has certainly pushed this farther than I would have dared. We will find something else to do . . . but no, I am now speechless as Janeen returns to the porch.

"Mom, will you take us swimming?"

I do not look at my mother. I can feel her eyes on us.

"Not now Janeen," Aunt Jeannette replies.

"Well, will you later?"

"Perhaps in a little while, Janeen."

"Well, when?"

"I don't know. Perhaps a little later."

"In a half-hour?"

"All right," says Aunt Jeannette wearily, *"in a half-hour."*

I look at Janeen. I am amazed at her power. This is something I have never considered—perhaps "no" doesn't mean "absolutely no.". . . It is a revelation.

The creek is still, with barely a breeze. We borrow a rowboat at the dock and my mother and aunt take turns rowing as we head out across the creek. Near the dock, the bottom is muddy and marshy, but as we move out toward the river, there are little sandbars and tiny coves that provide agreeable places to swim.

The edges of the island are always changing. There are some spots that look inviting from a distance, but when we move closer to shore we can see decaying tree stumps below the water's surface. At one time these places were above the tide long enough to support the growth of trees, but the creek has eaten at the shoreline, and the stumps now provide an anchorage for oysters and a hiding place for crabs.

We beach the rowboat on a clean stretch of sand and spend the afternoon here, our mothers sitting barefoot in the dry sand, Janeen and I splashing in the green-blue water. We are far from the dock. All that can be seen here is this spit of sand and the tiny line of green that is the distant shore. There are no boats within distance, no signs of civilization, no footprints other than our own. The world is mainly blue—the wide and broad expanse of water and sky.

The James Adams Floating Theatre

The James Adams Floating Theatre was the Chesapeake's version of a Mississippi showboat, though nowhere near as stylish as the elegant craft of America's western rivers. Built to withstand the unpredictable weather and wider expanses of water found on the Chesapeake, the *James Adams* was plain, boxy, and unadorned—a large barge-like boat housing a large auditorium, and she traveled to a succession of town docks throughout the summer season, bringing magic and glamour to the tidewater communities of the Eastern Shore.

The theatre was the creation of James Adams, who, along with his wife, had earlier careers as circus performers and carnival operators. Adams built the theatre on the hunch that the sort of showboat performances he had seen in the West would be a great hit in the entertainment-starved shore towns. He was right. The boat was immediately popular and its mixture of melodrama, westerns, and light comedies were shows to which "you can take your wife, mother, sweetheart, or children without blushing, but not without smiling."[51]

The arrival of the theatre, its bulky hulk towed from town landing to town landing, was usually heralded by an advance man who put up posters and announced the boat's impending appearance. Sometimes the musicians of the troupe would board a smaller boat and travel up the creeks and tributaries, announcing with their music the arrival of the *James Adams* at the local dock. Newspaper ads were also placed and free tickets were sent to automobile owners who would "use the tickets and bring a carload of paying customers." The showboat was such a tradition in tidewater towns that its arrival became a marker in the year's activities. People anticipated its yearly return, even using expressions such as "two years ago come showboat time or other similar expressions."[52]

The theatre, with a nineteen-foot-wide stage, could seat seven hundred guests in the general auditorium, boxes and balcony. It also contained dressing rooms and living space for the cast and orchestra who traveled with the theatre throughout a season that ran from spring through autumn.

Normally the showboat would spend a week at each of its stops, with a show every night except Sunday; sometimes a Saturday matinee would be included. Only the plays producing the highest box office receipts were repeated, and there was a different show each night. The main show would start at 8:15 P.M. Admission was thirty-five or forty cents. At 10:15 there was a concert or vaudeville show, which cost an additional ten or fifteen cents.[53]

Charles Hunter was the leading man of the showboat productions. James's sister, Beulah Adams, was billed as the "Mary Pickford of the Chesapeake," playing ingénue roles "well past 50 and when she was too plump for the part."[54] Plays such as *Pollyanna, Big Shot, Breakfast for One, Frisco Jenny, Man's Will, Woman's Way, The Mystic Isle, Little Lost Sister, Shooting Gold* and *Trail of the Lonesome Pine* were performed to the delight of the audience. The stories were of high moral character, celebrating the triumph of good over evil in their happy endings. At intermission the band would launch into effervescent tunes such as "I Wore a Big Red Rose," "Will You Be My Pony Boy," and "When You Wore a Tulip." While the current play was the main attraction for the evening, it was preceded by an audience "warm up" of jokes, music, and song.

"I remember the first time I got to go to the floating theatre. Your grandmother took Orville, Jeannette and I when the theatre was docked at Kent Narrows. It was thirty-five cents each to get in for the show— $1.40 for all of us, a lot of money in those days. We were seated in the balcony and they were going up and down selling Crackerjacks and Mom bought some for us. We had never had Crackerjacks before. I can still taste them! And a prize in each box! The man on stage was welcoming everyone with songs and jokes. He sang:

> *I see a woman sitting up there,*
> *She's in the third row and in the twelfth chair;*
> *She came here to laugh and smile,*
> *And brought with her a little child.*

The James Adams Floating Theater. (Kent Island Heritage Society)

We counted the rows and seats to discover that he was singing about my mother and sister! How exciting! The actor knew that we were there!"

In the early 1920s novelist Edna Ferber traveled with the troupe for several weeks, and many people feel that it was the Adams Floating Theatre she had in mind when writing her famous novel, *Showboat*. Kern and Hammerstein visited the theatre in the fall of 1926 and went on to write the music and lyrics of the Broadway show based on Ferber's novel.

> Ferber lived on the boat and soaked up all the stories and atmosphere she could. She watched the cook and her husband (Agnes and Joe) who became the basis for the fictional characters Queenie and Joe, who eventually were given the songs "Can't Help Lovin' Dat Man" and "Ol' Man River" respectively.[55]

The success of the musical led Adams to change his showboat's sign to read "The Original Floating Theatre." The theatre was then at the height of its popularity.

The arrival of silent films, radio, and talkies lessened interest in the theatre, and in 1930 Adams sold it to Nina Howard of St. Michaels, Maryland, who continued to operate it until 1941. But the times were

Myrtle Seymour's store (circa 1940).

changing. The steamboat era had ended and many docks and landings fell into disuse. The popularity of movies and radio continued to grow. And the Original Floating Theatre had passed her time. She was sold South and rumor was that she would resume her glamorous life as a showboat, but that was not to be. On November 14, 1941, she was destroyed by fire in the Savannah River.

Stores and Shopping

Sooner or later, as the days go by, something would be run out of in the kitchen, and my father would be sent off to the store. Myrtle's store is unlike the grocery stores in the city. There are no expansive plate glass windows, no weekly specials advertised in bright red letters, no neat aisles of well-stocked shelves and sparkling chrome.

The store is housed in a long, low building, its weathered siding decorated with worn metal signs advertising seed corn and Royal Crown Cola. Tall gasoline pumps sit at the edge of the small parking area of sand and oyster shell sprawling in the hot white light of the summer sun. A deep overhang stretches across the front of the building, shading the windows and entrance from the heat, and the worn and bat-

The same building, with structural changes and without gas pumps, 1999.

tered screened door opens into a cool dark interior that smells of hay and seeds and luncheon meat. Myrtle bought the store from Mr. Coursey (who was also the local barber), and his barber chair sits unused at the back of the store.

There is a bright red Coca-Cola cooler just inside the door, and my father would usually stop and buy us a soda, the icy bottle cold in my hands, beads of condensation dripping on sunburned toes.

Myrtle is lanky and rawboned; she wears flowered cotton dresses and little white anklets encased in sturdy shoes. Her glasses perch near the end of her nose, and she squints in a way that makes me wonder if she cannot see or if she is simply trying to keep her glasses from sliding off her nose. She greets us warmly and helps my father find his purchases. We eat sandwiches for lunch, so he is usually shopping for lunchmeats and cheeses or other perishables such as milk, eggs, or butter. Mom Mom's tiny Norge refrigerator doesn't hold a very large supply of anything, although we use the icebox on the porch to store things that don't spoil quickly.

In summer the iceman comes by once a week. His truck, imprinted with the words "Queenstown Ice Company," pulls up our lane in a cloud of dust and stops in the yard with a jolt.

The iceman is always in a hurry. I watch as he quickly pulls a large

Early photograph of John Taylor's store in Chester. (Rita Stowe)

block from the back of his truck with a heavy pair of tongs, heaves it over his shoulder and heads for the porch.

Sometimes we go to Myrtle's store for bread. More often it arrives on the "Rice's" bread truck which pulls into our lane one morning a week. The driver wears a crisply starched white uniform, and he carries onto the porch a tray of assorted baked goods for the ladies to make their selections. Much to my dismay, and despite repeated lobbying, they rarely buy sweets. Mainly we snack on the abundance of fruit that surrounds us or on the occasional confection Mom Mom produces in her kitchen. Her specialties are strawberry shortcake (with a cooked marshmallow topping), rolly-bolly (biscuit dough filled with fruit), lemon meringue pie (lemony tart with drifts of browned meringue), ginger cookies (thin and crispy), poor man's cake (dense and heavy with molasses and raisins), and peach cakes (yeast dough covered with sliced fruit, cinnamon, sugar and butter). Of course, the bakery man has nothing that good to offer.

My father has completed his shopping and we have finished our sodas. It is time to go back to the farm.

For many, many years, shopping on Kent Island meant a trip to a general store. There was Taylor's and Coursey's on Route 18 near Piney Creek Road, Benton's at the corner of Crab Alley Road, Kirwan's, and Price's down the road toward Devil's Dominion, and Grollman's, Frampton's, or the American Store in Stevensville.

When my mother was a girl, the closest shopping to the Nash farm was at Taylor's store. It was owned and operated by Mr. John W. Taylor and his wife, Miz Noiley (Enola).

There was a wood-burning stove and a spittoon in the center of the room and the walls were lined with wooden shelving and counters. In front of the counters were kegs of nails and screws and a board was placed across the kegs to form a bench where the local farmers would gather to talk. There was a phone on the back wall; an old-fashioned one that you rang up yourself. I think it was the only one for miles; no one I knew had a phone.

81

1911   Miss Lolita Bryan
              To M E Benton

Nov 21	1 Bbl flour 5 40 10 lb lard 1.40	6 80
	1 tin can 15 5 lb coffee 25 1 25	1 40
	6 Bars Soap 25 6 Bt g powders 25	50
	5 lb w Soda 10 2 lb Starch 14	24
	4½ yds gingham 36 5 yds india linen 80	1 16
	10 lb Sugar 75 5¼ lb meat 69	1 44
	½ dg Eggs 15 cotton 5 2 pr hose 25	45
	3½ yds outing 28 15 yds flour oil clothes	4 48
	2 pr hose 20 pr Rubbers 60 9½ lb meat 1 12	
	cheese 5 candy 1 Eggs cakes 2 Milk 16	55
Nov 28	1 dg pickles 10 2 Bars Soap 10	20
" 29	meat 86 c crackers 5 Eggs 34	
Dec 5	candy 2 pickles 18 9 lb meat 1 17	
" 6	2 lb Coffee 50 5 lb Sugar 35 crack 10	
	1 can tomatoes 10 pickle 5 soap 10	
	1 lb Butter 30 6½ lb meat 81 cheese 10	
	½ dg Eggs 17 1 lb Butter 30 candy 2	
	cand 5 13 1 can Tomatoes 10	
	½ lb cheese 10 ½ dg Eggs 16	
" 18	cheese 5 cakes 2 1 set nut picks 26	
	1 lb coffee 25 pickle 5 meat 80	
		26 50
	credit by cash	12 50
		14 00
Dec 24	1 Set glasses 30 2 Bars Soap 10	40
	1 glass pitcher 15 pins 5	20
	4½ lb meat 86 1 lb coffee 25	
	pr corsets 50 Jam lb lard 11	
	pickle 5 pencil 2 hook & eyes 3	
	9½ lb meat 123 1 lb coffee 25	
	Starch 5 soap 10 pickle 10	

Page from Miss Molly Benton's record book listing payments and purchases. (Kent Island Heritage Society)

Interior of John and Enola Taylor's store in Chester, Maryland. (Rita Stowe)

The store sold staples such as canned goods, flour, sugar, coffee, kegs of molasses, pickles, and coil oil. There was a refrigerator for meats and cheeses and once a week there was ice cream, which came all the way from Centreville, highly perishable and packed in ice and salt. There were sections for dry goods, notions, medications, school supplies, and hardware. And a glass display cabinet of penny candy.

But the best part came after Thanksgiving. Miz Noiley would put up a sort of stairstep shelf near the front door. On it were displayed all sorts of dolls and toys. We would have to stop by that store nearly every day just to see what new thing had been put out there. And we would long for things we knew we probably wouldn't get . . . but we were excited and hoping we'd get something for Christmas even if it wasn't as grand as some of the dolls or toys on those shelves.

Down the road at the corner of Route 18 and Crab Alley Road and right next to the Chester School was Miz Molly Benton's store. The layout was much the same as Taylor's store, with a stove at the center of the room and benches in front of the counters where customers would stop to visit. The items sold included the usual staples such as canned goods, coffee, sugar, and flour. But Miz Benton also sold yard goods, buttons, ribbons and lace, and spools of sewing thread. There were shoes and boots, underwear, stockings, and hats. And being located next to the school, Miz Benton also had a ready market for school supplies and penny candy.

> Starting at the counter on the west side of the store there was a cabinet which held dyes, then an old-fashioned coffee grinder, turned by hand. Also, the old scales were next. They were balanced by weights from one ounce to ten pounds. . . . On the south side counters we find the money drawer with a desk over it which held the record book. Mollie wrote the date, each purchase, price, and name of the purchaser.[56]

If we were out in the schoolyard and saw our wagon and Old Phoebe tied up to the rail at Miz Benton's, we would ask permission to run over there. We were hoping for a nickel to buy some of that penny candy!

On Crab Alley Road (now known as Dominion Road) was Tom Price's store. Begun by his father in 1903, Price & Son sold general merchandise but was especially known for wallpaper, paint, and home products.

Do you remember the glass tray that Mom Mom had in her kitchen cabinet? Well, that came from Price's store. We gave it to her for Christmas in 1926. Orville and Jeannette and I walked all the way down to Price's to buy that for her . . . a good two miles, I guess. We had saved up our money; I think it was about three dollars. We were so pleased with ourselves for being able to buy her a present.

Farther south toward Dominion was Kirwan's Store. Operated by

My own memories of Chester begin in the very early 1930s. Since we lived between Stevensville and Love Point, we did most of our "dealing" at Frampton's, the American Store, or Grollman's in Stevensville. However, if we needed wallpaper, the place to go was Price & Son in Chester. Tom and Elsie Price could calculate the amount of wallpaper you needed so precisely that you wouldn't have enough left over to line a bureau drawer and their prices were reasonable.[57]

State Senator James E. Kirwan, it included a general store as well as a saw mill and lumberyard. Coal, coil oil, kerosene, and gasoline were sold as well as other building materials such as bricks, nails, and glass.

While some articles were ordered by catalog or from stores in Baltimore, for the most part people in those days found everything they needed at the general store.

On August 7 and 8, 1953, Jimmie Short and his Silver Saddle Boys, "stars of stage, screen, TV and records"[58] were the featured attraction at the gala opening of the Kent Island Shopping Center.

The Kent Island giant development has been constructed by the David M. Nichols and Company. It covers almost ten acres with 1,300 foot frontage on U.S. Route 50. It's located just two miles from the Eastern End of the new Chesapeake Bay Bridge, between Stevensville and Chester, on the Northern side of the heavily traveled dual highway that leads to the ocean resorts in the fastest growing section of Queen Anne's County.[59]

The center, considered a showplace, included many new businesses as well as others that had abandoned their earlier locations for a spot in the new sprawl of the shopping center. It was only the beginning. Governor Theodore McKeldin, who attended the grand opening, spoke to the crowd about the future.

We must protect these highways. It is to your interest as business people and to the interest of the traveling public and of the State of Maryland. Establishments for the furnishings of services and the dispensing of merchandise are essential, and I know of no better way to provide such services and goods than through wisely planned and well-regulated shopping centers.[60]

No one, not even Mr. McKeldin, could have predicted the rampant growth that followed the construction of the Bay Bridge. The highway expansion of the early 1990s cut off the shopping center he lauded in his talk, and Route 50 is chock-a-block with fast-food restaurants and national chains.

I am going berry picking this morning. Mom Mom has given me the colander and I am off across the lawn, the grass whispering soft and damp against my feet. The day is already warm, the world steamy with sun and dew. I am a hunter, a gatherer.

The blackberries grow throughout the fields and along the edges of the woods. Their drawback, of course, is their thorns. I never emerge from these briars without scratches, but I am pleased that I have never failed to return to my grandmother without a colander brimming with fruit. The berries are a tribute. They are also remarkable to me because they are a gift of nature. Unplanted and untended, they produce in amazing abundance.

The sun climbs higher. I can feel its growing warmth on my shoulders and neck as I bend to pick from the lower branches. When I stand, a soft breeze cools my skin, and I see the grasses and wildflowers about me dip and bend, dancing on air currents like gulls above the bay. There are blue cornflowers, red clover, yellow cress and goldenrod, delicate Queen Anne's Lace, and clumps of daisies and fat black-eyed susans, their faces open to the sun. Butterfly peas with delicate pink blossoms creep along the sandy ground. The wind stirs the trees as well, rustling them like crushed taffeta, their branches swaying against the bright blue sky. Insects chirp in the tall grass; birds sing their morning songs. The field is a good place to be.

I fill the colander to heaping with sweet, dark berries and return once again, scratched but triumphant, to the porch. I judge berrying to be worth it—first, for the satisfaction of the gathering; second, for the joy of morning fields; third, for the opportunity to bring something to my grandmother.

Wars and Confrontations

After the conflict between Claiborne and Calvert subsided, the residents of Kent Island continued a path of self-sufficiency and individualism. The island was indisputably a part of the Maryland colony but isolation and the often solitary occupations of farming and working the water fostered a fierce sense of self-determination that would continue well into the future.

> Saint Mary's was the Catholic County; Anne Arundel was the Protestant stronghold; and Kent Island was the seat of detached independence which several times blazed into revolt.[61]

Despite this individualism, many islanders were full-fledged patriots, participating in both the American Revolution and the War of 1812. In July of 1776 the Council of Safety sent lead and gunpowder to island residents, and Frederic Emory noted that "there is a person on Kent Island who has repaired many guns for the militia, more particularly in the lock, and we are informed is well qualified for the business." Captain Edward Veazey's independent militia company was stationed at Kent Island, and two other companies, commanded by Captains Barnes and Eliott, were positioned there as well. "They were militia and in all probability raised in the neighborhood," noted Emory. "The greatest part of the Queen Anne's military force seems to have been stationed on Kent Island, which was most exposed to attack, and at the same time commanded the entrance to Chester River."[62]

Blunt's Warehouse, located at Great Neck and built for tobacco storage, housed troops anticipating attack from British forces in the bay.

There were exceptions to the rule, however. Some Eastern Shore watermen were Tories, siding with the British because of their hatred for the slave-holding gentry who owned the large tobacco plantations of the shore. They frequently provided supplies to the British and sometimes operated as pirates raiding American ships and plantations.

On the upper Eastern Shore the notorious "China" Clows raided bayside plantations in Queen Anne's County and liberated slaves. Captured in his home on Kent Island after a fierce gun fight, Clows was hanged by the Maryland militia in 1788.[63]

During the War of 1812, the government did not put an emphasis on the protection of Kent Island as was done during the Revolution, and the island was taken by the British on August 5, 1813. Approximately two thousand troops were landed, a battery built at Kent Narrows, and the island used as a base for forays to the mainland. Troops advancing from Kent Island were to connect with additional troops disembarking along the Wye River for marches on Queenstown and Centreville, but militia lying in wait at Slippery Hill ambushed the Wye River group and stopped the invasion. Trenches are still visible on property at the southwest corner of the intersection of Route 18 and Bennett Point Road.

Emory reports that prior to the Civil War, sentiment in Queen Anne's County "seems to have been strongly in favor of the preservation of the Union by all peaceable means."[64] In 1861, however, in expectation of the need to defend themselves against possible incursion by Union troops, the 38th Regiment called for male citizens between the ages of 18 and 45 to meet at various locations for the purpose of electing officers and tallying enrollment. Among companies mentioned were "G," or Chesapeake Rifles, of Kent Island, "B" of Stevensville, and "E," Weedon's Store, Kent Island.

While no significant military action took place at Kent Island, the nearby towns of Queenstown, Centreville, and Easton were subject to brief occupations, pilfering of supplies, and arrests of local citizens by Union troops. On at least one occasion, Kent Island was used as a landing site for Union cavalry transported from Annapolis for movements on Queenstown and confiscation of cannon owned by the Paca family. A story handed down through the Eareckson family of Kent Island tells of the arrival of some Union soldiers at the home of Benjamin Winchester Eareckson and his wife, Elizabeth White Eareckson.

> When the Yankee soldiers demanded that she prepare a turkey dinner for them, Miss Betsey, as she was called, disregarded all the rules of Southern hospitality and chased the rascals out of the yard with a horsewhip.[65]

In 1917 island residents successfully defended themselves against the United States government and a federal plan to turn their home into a military proving ground. World War I was raging in Europe, and the War Department, intent on the development of new weaponry, decided that Kent Island was the most viable space on the East Coast for ordnance testing. The secretary of war declared that those living on the island would have to leave their homes, and some residents signed options on their properties, feeling they had no choice but to acquiesce. On Monday, July 9, 1917, residents met to try to save the island. The crowd swelled in response to the call for alignment against the federal plan. Intending at first to use Legg's Hall in Stevensville, the plan was abandoned and the meeting moved to the yard of Christ Church.

> Brave little Kent Island is preparing (by every honorable means) to fight the invasion of her shores. Monday afternoon a rousing mass meeting was held in the churchyard of the Episcopal Church.[66]

"The Committee of 100" worked through the next day collecting signatures on a petition protesting the planned takeover. Known as "The Kent Island Home Preservation Committee," representatives boarded the Maryland, Delaware, and Virginia train for a trip to Washington and a meeting with the secretary of war.

> The people of the Island are ready and willing to sacrifice their homes to bring about a victory in the event of war, but feel that if

The Kent Island Home Preservation Committee visited Washington, D.C., protesting plans to convert their island to an ordnance proving ground. They presented their petition to Secretary of War Newton Diehl Baker in July 1917. (Kent Island Heritage Society)

the government wishes to establish a proving ground, they should select some less densely populated section or a section which is not so fertile and valuable as a food producing center. The people of Kent Island stand ready and willing to make any sacrifice that the government may deem necessary, but as they understand the situation, the present plans have nothing to do with the successful prosecution of the war. They are, therefore, opposed to the proposition of losing the homes and businesses it has taken them a lifetime to build up.[67]

The strong opposition of the islanders persuaded the War Department to abandon their plans. Kent Island was left to prosper and the ordnance proving ground was established instead at Aberdeen, in Harford County.

During World War II, there was concern that enemy planes might attempt to destroy the aircraft and supply factories near Baltimore. A number of Kent Island residents volunteered as civil defense workers. Uncle Orville and Aunt Katherine worked as airplane spotters from a site on the mainland, watching the sky and reporting all aircraft activity. Numerous young men from Kent Island served in both the European Theater and the Pacific during World War II. Many of them lost their lives.

Down near the start of Piney Road is Aunt Lil's place. She has a small white two-storied home and next to it a rambling line of connecting buildings that once housed her infamous dancehall and tavern. Lil is the second wife and widow of my grandfather's brother William and the shame of our family.

"She ran a dancehall and a tavern down there for the darkies. It was a rough place, especially on Friday and Saturday nights."

"She didn't care what she did. If a couple people didn't finish their beers, she'd pour them together and sell 'em to somebody else."

"During Prohibition she used to go up to Baltimore in an old Model T. She'd buy booze and bring it back in medicine bottles. Drove all the way around the bay, up through Elkton. She had an accident once, drove right into a ditch. The police helped her out but never looked into the car. Oh, she had nerve!"

The small white house is closed up, the curtains drawn. Aunt Lil lives in Florida which reportedly has a better climate for her asthma. My grandmother is not sad about this. Her dislike for Aunt Lil has always been obvious, something I have noted with interest as I have never known my grandmother to speak ill of others. No amount of questioning has sated my curiosity. I am simply told that I am too young to hear such things, that Aunt Lil is a wicked woman, a woman who has done evil things for money, a woman she will not claim as any relative of hers.

My grandmother is Episcopalian, not an old-time Methodist. The dancehall and tavern, while certainly objects of disapproval, are not enough to justify the censure I hear in her voice.

The line of buildings that were once the dancehall-tavern are empty now, the doors unlocked, a few window panes missing, the yard a jumble of weeds and untrimmed shrubbery. Janeen and I have never been particularly interested in this rundown place, but now that we know that Aunt Lil is a wicked woman, we are curious about it.

"Don't you two go down there."

"That building is old and has been empty a long time."

"The floorboards are probably rotten and could give way on you — you could get seriously hurt."

"Coons get into empty buildings to nest. A coon on its hind legs is as tall as you!"

"And vicious if they're cornered or defending their young."

"And sometimes a hobo will put up in an old empty building. You could get carried off and we wouldn't know!"

We are not afraid. And besides, we are bored today. We will just take a walk, maybe pass the building, maybe look in through a window. Certainly there is no harm in that.

The building is quite dilapidated; the grass and weeds are deep and high. And it is still here . . . quiet and unnerving with only the sound of a breeze, a birdcall. We creep across the yard, stepping carefully onto the rickety porch to peer through the window. It is dark inside and the windowpanes are so dirty that we cannot see much at all. Perhaps we could open the door and just go a little way inside.

The interior is dim and shadowy, with cobwebs and dust everywhere. We walk carefully (mindful of floorboards), but discover that the place is disappointingly empty, absent of useable treasure or any clue regarding Aunt Lil's wickedness. There are a few chairs scattered about and against one wall a large old jukebox, gaudy and ornate, draped in cobwebs, silent for years.

We discuss in whispers whether we are brave enough to venture upstairs. The adult stories of floorboards and coons are enough to deter us, so we continue to tiptoe about the downstairs, speaking in whispers, making each other increasingly nervous. And then, a bang

The abandoned building that was Lil Nash's Dance Hall, in Chester, Maryland. (Author's photo)

on the back window, a bloodcurdling scream, a patchy green face with a drooling mouth. We run in terror out of the building, across the porch and into the yard, headed full speed for the road.

We are stopped by the sound of laughter.

It is my brother, Gary, with leaves all over his face, howling with laughter in the backyard.

Railroads

The first railroad to serve Kent Island was the Queen Anne's Railroad. The company was established in 1894 with the ambitious goal of developing rail and steamboat service from Baltimore to the beaches of Delaware. In constructing the Queen Anne's Railroad the company set itself in competition with larger and more established lines and invoked the opposition of giants like the Baltimore and Eastern Shore Railroad, already in operation on the shore, and the Pennsylvania Railroad, which feared competition with its Cape May line. The officers of the company forged ahead with their plan, however, and the first track was laid from Queenstown to Lewes, Delaware, in 1896–98. In 1902 it was extended westward over Kent Narrows to Love Point at the northernmost tip of Kent Island. Love Point provided an excellent harbor and was closer to Baltimore than the Queenstown pier. The construction of the railroad was, of course, the impetus for the development of the Love Point resort.

The Queen Anne's Railroad enjoyed several years of expansion and growth, but ultimately suffered unforeseen misfortune and financial difficulties.

> The winter of 1903–1904 brought a devastating cold wave which blocked all bay traffic for nearly a month.* On February 8, 1904 a large area of Baltimore's commercial district was laid in ruins by fire. These incidents caused dire consequences to be felt on the Queen Anne's Railroad, since most of its revenue came from the Baltimore end.[68]

The railroad went into receivership, and in 1905 it was sold to the Maryland, Delaware, and Virginia Railroad, a newly incorporated arm of the Pennsylvania Railroad, the company that had opposed the building of the Queen Anne. The Pennsy system continued to operate the line through the "golden age" of Love Point and the demise of steamboat travel.

The Pennsylvania added more stops, and the train now passed through stations at Stevensville, Chester, and Kent Narrows as it crossed the island. Locals used the train for transportation, but also as a means of moving seafood and produce to the Love Point steamers for the trip to the markets of Baltimore.

---

*This was the winter that my grandfather's letters were not received in Baltimore, almost ending my grandparents' romance.

Kent Narrows, Kent Island, Md.

1931-32

Postcard made in 1931–32 showing the Kent Narrows bridges. (Betty Shulz)

Students from Grasonville (once Winchester) would board the train to Stevensville in order to attend high school.

> Evelyn King Reese . . . had to walk from her home to the railroad station in Grasonville, a distance of a mile and a half. She then rode the train to Stevensville, and walked from there to the school.[69]

The growth of the automobile as American's choice in transportation doomed even the mighty Pennsylvania system. Services were cut and finally halted on Kent Island, the last train running to Chester on November 23, 1956.

> Passenger service ended in 1938. Hurricane Hazel rendered the Kent Narrows Bridge unusable in 1954 and the line west of Queenstown was formally abandoned in 1956.[70]

Undated early twentieth-century photograph of Kent Narrows Bridge. (Betty Shulz)

Uncle Orville is the only one of my uncles who has worked as a waterman all his life; crabbing and grass shrimping in summer, oystering in winter. He built his own boat, the *Miss Kitty,* and he builds crab pots and carves duck decoys for hunting.[71] Uncle Orville is a shy, quiet man with a face weathered by the Chesapeake. He has a wide, warm smile that lights his face and crinkles his eyes.

Recently, he has taken up a new career. He and Aunt Katherine have bought a little drive-in restaurant on the mainland, selling submarine sandwiches, hamburgers, hot dogs. and soft ice cream. The restaurant is up Route 50; a small, low wooden building, painted orange and white, it stands in a sandy parking area next to a gas station. The roof extends outward from the building to protect the clusters of outside tables and benches from sun and rain, and there are two little sliding glass windows through which the customers can place and receive their orders. They have a lot of business from the truckers who now travel over the bridge.

Glossy pictures of tempting food decorate the jalousie windows—burgers with dripping, melted cheese, dew-kissed lettuce and perfect tomato slices; hot dogs topped with perfect dabs of mustard and minced pickle; ice cream sundaes swimming in chocolate, butterscotch, crushed pineapple, or strawberry sauces and topped with whipped cream and glistening maraschino cherries; banana splits nestled in little blue plastic boats, a large smiling banana looming over the colorful poster.

We are important honored guests and are allowed inside the back door. The storage room is soon bursting with relatives, boxes, shelves, and freezers. My tiny grandmother is ensconced in the only chair, surrounded by family, everyone chattering and talking as Aunt Katherine and Uncle Orville work. I am soon bored with these adults and wander outside to survey the glossy pictures of the various sandwiches and ice cream fantasies that decorate the windows. Uncle Orville's face looks as sunny and friendly as ever, so perhaps he is happy here, frying hamburgers and making ice cream sundaes.

The highway stretches out in front of the parking lot like a soiled, oily ribbon; trucks speed by, sending up clouds of dust, the breeze bringing the gasoline scent of the service station and road to my nose. I think instead of the creek, where the only noise is of a boat moving through cool water, or the birds calling from the pinewoods and marsh. The creek, where a breeze brings refreshment, soft against hot skin; the creek, where the smells are of marsh and grass and salt . . .

Uncle Orville leaving the water!

My mother says that you could hardly blame him. The life of a waterman is hard work, with long hours in the sun, wind, and cold, with some years good, some bad, your success depending on more than your will and intentions. But still, I wonder whose idea this was, and if he misses the freedom and the pattern of life given by boat and bay and wind.

I am bothered by this; it is as though a death-knell has been rung that I do not understand. I do not trust these changes and am saddened, uneasy at some approaching unchosen fate. Uncle Orville leaving the water!

I look at the slick pictures in the windows, each one looking more delicious, more tantalizing, more succulent than the last. I am not sure what I should choose. I have learned not to trust such pictures; no matter what I choose, it will not be exactly like the picture, and there will always be a picture more scrumptious than my choice.

Kent Narrows

Kent Island nestles close against Maryland's Eastern Shore and is separated from the mainland by Kent Narrows, a fast rush of saltwater known to sailors as a dangerous and swift stretch of tide. The water of the Narrows was once much shallower. Historical references allude to the site as the "Wading Place":

> A locality spoken of in the Court Records for 1719 as the Wading
> Place on the east side of Kent Island, and near Wading Place Bay

Undated photograph of a baptism ceremony at Kent Narrows. (Betty Shulz)

(the present Eastern Bay?), would seem to have been the ford used by persons in passing from Kent Island to the mainland.[72]

Many years ago there was also a ferry service here. Passengers traveling northward, for example, would take the ferry from Annapolis to Broad Creek, disembark, and cross the island to board the Kent Narrows ferry for the short trip to the mainland and the continuation of their journey. The Kent Narrows ferry lost substantial business when the Broad Creek line ceased operation, and eventually closed.

There wasn't any ferry there when I was young. But we called it that all the same. If someone was going down to Kent Narrows, they would always say they were going "down the ferry" and we would know just what they meant.

Emory notes that mention of the Wading Place was made in the Upper House Proceedings of 1671 and in an agreement dated April 16, 1723, to "causeway the marsh that leads from the ferry at the Wading Place, next to Kent Island, all along from said ferry the usual road that leads from said ferry unto the extent of said marsh, to the fast land, the direct way to Queens Town." The causeway was to be thirteen feet wide at the bottom and ten feet wide at the top and reinforced with logs and poles "where needful in some soft or miry places." This causeway obstructed any traffic through the Narrows, and in 1874 the legislature approved funds for the removal of the causeway and the construction of the first true bridge.[73]

Some of the current width and depth of the Narrows may be the result of natural erosion but most of it was created by a series of dredging operations by the Army Corp of Engineers, begun with the removal of the old causeway. The primary reason for opening up the Narrows was to create deep-water access for travel from the Chester River to Eastern Bay without the necessity of circling the island. Several bridges have crossed the Narrows over the years; my mother said that the newest bridge is the fourth in her lifetime.

I remember that old, old bridge. Mr. Joe Burns used to turn it with a forked stick to open it up. And the least amount of water, that bridge got covered! Once, when we were in school, the tide came up and the kids from Grasonville couldn't get home. The teacher said "Find a friend to stay with tonight" and that was that. Their parents knew not to expect them coming home.

Opened in 1990, the newest bridge arches sixty-five feet above the Narrows providing an uninterrupted flow of vehicular traffic. The old drawbridge, dwarfed by its successor, still functions in its shadow.

The new bridge was part of $87 million package of changes completed in the early 1990s that drastically changed traffic patterns on Kent Island. The primary purpose of the new plan was to relieve the congestion of summer traffic, to get people to the beaches with less inconvenience.

A flood during high tide slows traffic in 1950. (Betty Shulz)

When the entire project is finished, the five existing traffic signals will be removed and 15 primary intersections will either be modified or eliminated, according to John Contestabile, an SHA project development chief.[74]

The cost was year-long inconvenience to people that live on the island, many of whom refer to it as the "Columbus Highway," meaning it is a road on which you must travel West to go East.

Kent Narrows has also seen a succession of railroad bridges, but they, too, have long since disappeared, the last one demolished by Hurricane Hazel in 1954. In my childhood the mainland shore was bordered with oyster-packing houses, rows of shanties, and the beginnings of the Fisherman's Inn. The island side of the Narrows was exclusively salt marsh. It was filled in and macadamized, and a mall was built on it in the 1980s. Today, the businesses and buildings of my childhood have been largely replaced by restaurants, marinas, and inns.

The original Fisherman's Inn, in 1934. (Betty Shulz)

Fisherman's Inn

Captain Alex Thomas was born on Kent Island in 1901. In November 1986 the *Queen Anne's Record-Observer* featured a profile of this Kent Island waterman:

> I hunted and trapped all 442 acres of this marsh since I was a kid and I knew every inch of it. It was filled with black ducks and soft crabs.

As a boy, Thomas worked hard. Like many other boys, he began working on the water at an early age in order to help support his family. And following the pattern of many young island men, he left his home to seek a better paying job in the city, only to return, answering the irresistible call of the water and the island way of life. *The Shoreman* of March 1985 quotes Thomas:

Loading empty oyster shells at Thomas's Packing House. The shells will be dumped to create new oyster beds. (Betty Shulz)

There weren't many boys my age who didn't start working then, working to help their families. . . . I was a waterman until I was 24, and then I moved to Baltimore. Worked over there and saved my money and came back here and bought this piece of ground right on the Narrows. And I went back onto the water.

Captain Alex and his wife built a small frame house with a screened front porch at the edge of the marsh and moved in with their young family. Route 18, a dirt track and the only road crossing from Kent Island to the Narrows, was just outside their door. Captain Alex started right into crabbing and oystering, hunting duck and trapping muskrat. He also installed gas pumps in front of his home, intending to make extra dollars by selling Atlantic gasoline to people passing over the old bridge. Travelers, frequently hungry and thirsty, began to inquire after a place to eat, and May Thomas began selling food.

If a person came in and wanted pork chops, for example, Miz May

Rows of luxury boats form a backdrop for a remnant of the shanties surviving at Kent Narrows. (Author's photo)

would walk down to Lottie Chance's store and get the chops and bring them back and cook it up for them.

The Thomases picked crab and shucked oysters in season, and would oblige travelers by selling crab cakes, softshell crabs, or oyster sandwiches when they stopped for gas. There were few places to stop for gas or prepared foods in 1930, and the trip from Baltimore to the Shore was a long one. Their reputation grew and the business grew, and Captain Alex added a packinghouse. The packinghouse sat closer to the water, and—like other packinghouses—was reached by a series of planks laid across the marsh. *The Shoreman* article continues:

> We were about the only place between here and Ocean City where you could get a sandwich. We started the seafood business a couple of years after that.

Thomas commented in the November 1986 *Observer*: "Work, work,

The old drawbridge is dwarfed by the new Kent Narrows Bridge, built to speed traffic from the city to the ocean. (Author's photo)

work. That's all we did. We sold oysters for seventy-five cents a gallon to Baltimore."

By 1939 the house was getting cramped. Captain Alex, Miz May, son Harold, and daughter Betty lived in half of the little house, running the restaurant from the other side. Captain Alex wanted to expand, but the bank turned down the loan, rejecting his marshy land as collateral. He eventually borrowed four hundred dollars from a friend in order to add on a second floor, install two bathrooms (he said the outhouse had floated away on a high tide), and enlarge the porch. The first floor was now completely given over to the restaurant, with family quarters on the second floor. In the summer, Captain Alex and Miz May would sometimes rent their bedrooms to fishermen, and the family would move temporarily to the porch to sleep. Eventually, Captain Alex built a row of tiny cabins, renting them to travelers or fishermen for three dollars a night.

In 1950 the Kent Narrows Channel was dredged and the sand and muck used to fill in the marsh between the restaurant and the packinghouse. A long side porch was added, increasing restaurant capacity to 130.

In 1971, Captain Alex, along with his daughter Betty and her husband Oscar "Sonny" Schulz, built a new and modern Fisherman's Inn on the property. That building was totally destroyed by fire in December of 1980 but was rebuilt on the same foundation. It reopened in 1981 and continues today as a Kent Narrows landmark. The restaurant dining room seats 250, larger and more successful than anything Captain Alex and Miz May imagined when they built their little house at the edge of the marsh.

Uncle Robert is an electrician by trade, and he has a truck with "Nash Electric" printed in big letters on its side. He, too, left the island as a young man but he did not stay away for long. He does not like the city and says it is not normal to live in a place where people burrow into the ground and stick out their heads like muskrats.

He is an intelligent, thoughtful man with soft brown eyes. I am always welcome with him; he likes children and plays with and teases us, all to our complete delight.

Uncle Robert is the king of the lawnmowers and their murderer as well. Conquering fields and shearing lawns, lawnmowers are driven to death at the hands of Uncle Robert. They disappear with great regularity and are replaced with bigger, stronger models. He cuts grass in the evening, the whole world made fragrant with chopped blades of grass. Into twilight the mower hums onward, the scent of new-mown grass heavy on the air, the sky darkening, the fireflies flashing. Armed with a bamboo rake, I have been following along behind him, raking the clippings into little stacks that are now scattered about the yard.

Mom Mom has been calling from the porch for at least the last half hour.

"Robert, stop now; you'll work yourself to death."

The mower drones on.

"Robert, stop now. The mosquitoes must be eating you alive."

He cannot hear her over the drone of the mower, but returns her wave as he passes, the mower headed outward to make another sweep across the velvet lawn.

"Robert, you've done enough now," she entreats as he once again passes the porch. "You'll work yourself to death. Come in on the porch and have a cold drink."

Uncle Robert continues mowing. She sends me running out across the wide yard to flag him down. He knows why I am there, waves to me cheerfully, shakes his head, and continues to cut grass.

It is getting too dark to cut grass," she complains. "I don't know how you can see what you are doing."

I think this is a game they play. She knows he will not stop until he wants to, nor will he come onto the porch. He will lean against the screened panel ledge and talk with us after he is satisfied with his job. She pretends exasperation, but I think she is secretly pleased by his tenacity, by his determination to give her this freshly cut lawn.

The mower drones on. I struggle along with my rake, heaping up great piles of grass, with never a chance to catch him. I admire his heart; if he will not quit, then neither will I.

Sundays are not the same as other days. They are slower, softer, as though the very air has grown more dense and the universe is breathing in long, slow breaths. It is as if a blanket has been thrown over the day, muffling all but the occasional call of a bird. We sit in the still heat of the porch, mesmerized by the heartbeat of the day. We hear the soft crunch of oyster shells, as Uncle Robert's Dodge pulls slowly up the lane and into the front yard.

"Come on," he calls from his seat behind the wheel. "Let's go for a drive."

He and Aunt Minnie wait while we get ourselves ready. Mom Mom removes her apron, brushes my hair and locks the almost-never-locked kitchen door with a big ancient key that she hides on top of the medicine cabinet.

I have been on many Sunday drives, but never like the ones we take with Uncle Robert. He takes us down roads that my grandmother never knew existed, through sleepy towns, past abandoned home-steads, churches, farms, and manors; past stretches of marsh and long sandy beaches, to graveyards and historic sites. We have traveled from Love Point to Kent Point, from the Chesapeake to Kent Narrows and beyond. He has shown me the site of Indian graveyards he used to explore as a boy, the cliffs now eroding into the Bay. We have walked through the ruins of the old Anglican church at Broad Creek, where only remnants of a brick foundation and a few headstones remain. We have driven past farms and manors draped in history: Cloverfields, Friendship, Crayford, Goose Point, Indian Springs, Scillen, Stevens Adventure. At Stevensville I learn that the two-storied white-framed antique shop was the school my family attended: elementary classes on the first floor, the high school upstairs. We drive past Christ Church, the Episcopalian parish where our family was baptized and confirmed.

We travel off the island as well, to Centreville, Easton, and Chestertown; to the historic village of Wye Mills, where flour was ground for Washington's troops at Valley Forge and where we wander through the graveyard of the church, reading marker stones. We stop to see the Old Wye Oak, Maryland's official state tree, a magnificent spreading white oak that is estimated to be five centuries old.

We have been to St. Michaels, with its maritime museum and light-house; and once, when all of us were sure he did not know where he was, he delighted us with a ride on the tiny ferry that crosses the Tred Avon River to the historic town of Oxford.

Wherever we roam, I can be sure that we will eventually arrive at Uncle Orville's drive-in, and complete our journey with some ice cream fantasy. We travel back to the farm, the day spent, the sky grown dark, tomorrow waiting. He keeps his headlights shining onto the porch while Mom Mom locates the key and unlocks the door. The familiar porch and house receive us and we climb the stairs to bed. Outside my window the branches of the walnut tree move in the breeze, an owl hoots from the woods, the crickets sing, and I am content and safe and soon asleep.

Christ Church Parish

As William Claiborne established his settlement, he built a stockade, a store, and a church, a congregation of the Church of England. In 1632, Claiborne brought the Reverend Richard James to serve as his community's first rector. Claiborne's expense records show payments to two other ministers as well as the purchase of bibles and prayer books.

It is not known how seriously Claiborne practiced his religion. The establishment of the church may well have been for the purpose of making his claim to Kent Island legitimate. In the seventeenth century, the definition of a "settled" colony required the presence of a church. Some historians have offered that Claiborne's church existed only as a means of giving his settlement authority, should a conflict with the Calverts come to pass.

Little is known of the early church buildings. The services were most likely held initially at the fort or in a private home, although there are historical references to a separate structure as early as 1636 or as late as 1652. Clarence Gould describes the building of the church:

> In 1636 Claiborne supervised the "framing" of a church. This obviously refers to a regular church structure, but it does not necessarily mean that the building was set up and sheathed. There is a persistent tradition that a church was built in 1649, 1650, or 1652, depending on the narrator, and some writers add the details that it was built of brick and located at Broad Creek. The more cautious modern historians, however, are unwilling to commit themselves to anything beyond the fact that some church existed on the Island in early years. It was referred to in 1692 and described in 1714 as "old and very much gone to decay."[75]

Some historians reasonably question the reference to the Broad Creek location because it would seem unlikely for a church to be located so far north of the original settlement and fort. This might indicate that settlement moved up the island perimeter more quickly than was supposed, for Clarence Gould aptly points out that when the "new" church was built at Broad Creek in 1712, there is no mention of a change in location.

Over the years, Christ Church was plagued with a number of difficulties, among them financial problems, low attendance, scarcity of adequate clergy, and the denominational differences with the ruling Catholic Calverts. Yet from the time of the construction of the 1712 building at Broad Creek until the American Revolution, the parish seems to have experienced a period of growth and stability. A rectory was built, a glebe established, and a tax levied on tobacco allowing for improvement monies. The congregation grew substantially, and an ell was added to the original structure to accommodate them.

Historians Emory and Gould contend that the American Revolution brought a quick downward turn in the church's prosperity. Throughout the new republic, they suggest, the Anglican Church was generally abandoned by its congregations because of the close association with the British throne.

> Although the Revolution was definitely a civil war in this country, when it was over almost everybody, even most of those who had supported the British cause, accepted the decision of arms and developed an antagonism to England and all things English. The Anglican Church was very English, and although it officially broke all foreign connections and became the Protestant Episcopal Church of the United States, there long remained a feeling that it was tainted with Toryism.[76]

Christ Church was maintained by a few families, although the pulpit was often vacant, and over the decades the building fell into serious disrepair. In 1820, the Reverend Purnell F. Smith visited the vacant parishes on the Eastern Shore and recorded the following impression.

> On the 7th went into Queen Anne's county and on the 10th passed over to Kent Island. Here I found the church in a very deplorable

Christ Church, Stevensville, Maryland. (David Prencipe, MdHS)

state. The house is not fit to preach in. The pulpit is pulled down, and all the pews are taken away by some of the neighboring inhabitants, as well as many of the bricks out of the wall, and stock of all kinds take shelter in the church. . . . I preached in a meeting house to a tolerably large congregation. But I believe there was not a prayerbook in the house beside my own. . . . as to repairing the church, at the present time they think it could not be done. I advised them to set about repairing it immediately, and several of them expressed a wish to do so, but I fear it will not be done.[77]

Five years later, in 1825, Reverend Jackson of Chestertown filed a similar report:

> We found the affairs of that parish in a deplorable condition. . . .
> The church is almost in ruins, and the funds appears to be miser-
> ably mismanaged. . . . we urged them to repair the church, though
> I fear there is not much prospect of the congregation being re-
> vived.[78]

The decline continued until the appearance of a Mr. Matthias Harris, an energetic lay reader who took on the revival of the Christ Church
parish. Upon reaching Kent Island, he wrote to the bishop that "he
found the church in a deplorable condition" and the congregation as
"sheep without a shepherd" yet through perseverance he managed to
raise money and hire workmen for the repair of the building. They
determined that the original section was completely ruined, but the ell
that was added before the Revolution seemed repairable. Matthias later
reported:

> In one hour our hopes were laid low, our joy was turned into
> mourning, our rejoicing into heaviness of heart. . . . The walls of
> the old part were in so ruinous a state that it was deemed advis-
> able to pull [it] down and repair the new part, which seemed
> much stronger. . . . After the workmen had pulled down the old
> part, and whilst they were engaged in clearing away the rubbish,
> etc., the roof of the remaining part fell in, pushing out the walls
> in each side, and thus blasted our fondest expectations.[79]

Matthias, saddened but undeterred, proceeded with limited funding
to build a new sanctuary. By 1870 that hastily built church was in
disrepair. Additionally, the Broad Creek location was no longer the
center of activity that it had been during the heyday of the ferry service.
The town of Broad Creek had essentially drifted northward to become
part of Stevensville, and the membership decided that if they were
going to rebuild they would do so at that site. In 1880 the sanctuary at

Broad Creek was demolished, and the Victorian structure in Stevensville was built. It is believed that foundation stones used in the 1880 structure date from the 1712 church at Broad Creek.

Towns & Villages

The towns of Kent Island have interesting names, the significance of many lost to history. Chester likely earned its name from its proximity to the Chester River. Prior to using that name, the area was known as Sharktown and appears as such on an undated map.[80]

Along Route 18, the smaller and colorfully named villages of Buzzardsville, Hell's Kitchen, and Ticktown were established. I have heard from several sources that the origin of the name "Buzzardsville" came about because the local men, who dressed mainly in black, had the custom of sitting on a fence outside the general store to talk and smoke. Someone commented that they looked like a bunch of buzzards sitting there. The name was born and stuck, at least until modern times. There has also been discussion in the present day as to the proper name of Dominion, though old-timers will inform you that the name Devil's Dominion is long-standing and possibly with good reason.

The community of Broad Creek grew up around the original ferry landing and was by far the largest town on the island. The 1871 volume of the *State Gazette for Maryland and District of Columbia* notes the names of fifty-three persons of varying occupations within the town of Broad Creek. Listed are several general stores, shoemakers, milliners, a mantua maker, a jeweler, a postmaster and constable, tanners, wheelwrights, blacksmiths, harness makers, carpenters, school teachers, physicians, ministers, and undertakers. In addition, seventy-six farmers are listed for the general area of Broad Creek. The same *Gazette* lists Stevensville only as "a post office on Kent Island, at the head of Coxe's Creek,"[81] with a list of twenty-six area farmers but no mention of operating businesses. The Kent Island Heritage Society notes that the town was founded in 1850, the land given by the two Stevens family brothers for whom it was named.

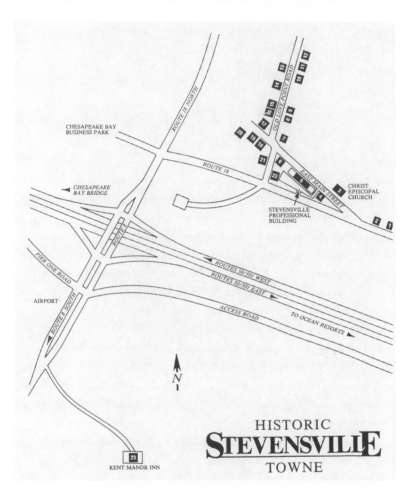

Routes 50 and 301 on Kent Island bypass the historic town of Stevensville. (Kent Island Heritage Society)

When the newly established ferry service from Annapolis to Rock Hall brought about a major decline in the number of traveling customers, many people from Broad Creek migrated northward to the newly formed town of Stevensville. Soon the largest community on the island, Stevensville became a center of trade for both farmers and watermen. With the coming of the steamboat era, and the establishment of the railroad, Stevensville enjoyed increasing prosperity as a result of its location along a major transportation route connecting the Eastern and Western Shores. The growing town contained a variety of stores, a car dealership & garage, doctor's offices, a hotel, two churches, a bank and post office, the island high school, an opera house, and a number of attractive homes of late-nineteenth and early-twentieth-century design.

In preparation for the increased traffic that the new Chesapeake Bay Bridge would bring to the island, the State of Maryland constructed a new highway south of Stevensville. The completion of the bridge in 1952 precipitated a sprouting of commercial development along the new thoroughfare (Route 50/301) and the center of commerce was suddenly removed from the town. The demise of the railroad dealt another economic blow, and Stevensville—once a thriving center of business—became a quiet backwater, with empty buildings and little traffic.

The highway's bypassing of the town is seen as a blessing in disguise today. The rapid development along the highway left the village in a time warp, untouched by fast-food outlets, gas station marts, and chain stores. Stevensville remains significantly unchanged since the early part of the twentieth century and contains a number of fine buildings built between 1840 and 1915. In 1988, Bethesda developer Roger Eisinger established the Stevensville Limited Partnership. Working in association with the Kent Island Heritage Society, a long-range plan was developed for the restoration of historic buildings and the attraction of new businesses. Though now significantly gentrified, Stevensville is a charming example of a turn-of-the-century Eastern Shore town, and has been placed on the National Register of Historic Places.

Stevensville High School

The first Stevensville High School was built in 1909, housing both the grammar school for Stevensville and the first high school in the area. It was a one-story building of frame construction containing four rooms. In 1913 a second story was added, with the expanding high school

"The boys played better here than anywhere that season," reads a note on the 1931 photograph (above). "Lost by one point. Roger Denny would not get in the picture. He was one of the good players. In fact they were all good, and how!" Left to right, Ben Jewell, Bill Eaton, Peck Thompson, Mathew Haspert, Walton Thompson, Jimmy White, Vernon Clark, Bright Price.

The 1929 State Volleyball Champions. Left to right: Mary Frances Tanner, Isabel Fairbanks, Mary Palmer, Leah Grollman, Edna Reamy, Madeline Clark, Florence Baxter, Vernice White.

A note on this photograph reads: "This picture was taken at noon one day in our last year at Stevensville High School [1931]. Girls played against boys in baseball, score 3 to 3 . . . some team and how!" Left to right, Dot Lewis, Lib Stallings, Dot Taylor, Catherine Kirwan, Margaret Nash, Julia Norman, Ruth Kolata, Alma Thompson, Evelyn Ewing, Dot Stevens, Delma Coleman, A. Gardner, E. Harris. Virginia King, and Lib Jones, at far left.

The former Stevensville High School. (David Prencipe, MdHS)

occupying the second floor while the grammar school classrooms remained on the first. The school drew students from all over the island as well as a portion of the mainland.

J. Fred Stevens was the highly respected principal of the high school and he served in that position for twenty-nine years. He also taught classes, primarily general science, geometry, and chemistry. When school let out for the summer, J. Fred worked from farm to farm, helping the local farmers with the threshing of winter wheat.

J. Fred didn't put up with any nonsense. He wanted you to get an education. I was in his class for plane geometry. He would say "I bet Margaret could do it," and I would stay up late working by the oil lamp, trying to figure out a problem so Mr. Stevens wouldn't be disappointed in me.

Extracurricular activities included plays, dinners, and musical events such as "Class Night," a special production by the senior class. The James Whitcomb Riley Literary Society and the Henry Wadsworth Longfellow Literary Society sponsored debates, recitations, readings, and monologues. Sports were popular, particularly baseball, volleyball, fieldball, and soccer. In 1929, the female volleyball team from Stevensville progressed through the regional divisions to win the state championship. The team boarded the Love Point ferry for the trip to Baltimore; they were housed at Towson State Teachers' College and played their championship game at Municipal Stadium.

A new brick high school was begun in 1930. The original frame schoolhouse continued as an elementary school but ultimately was used for other purposes. For many years the structure housed an antique shop. A more recent renovation subdivided the space for office use, and it is now known as "Old Schoolhouse Commons."

The Garden of Eden

Uncle Bill lives in Baltimore. He works for the Baltimore Gas and Electric Company, but in his heart and soul he is a waterman. I hardly ever see Uncle Bill except in summer, when he and Aunt Lollie spend several weeks at the farm. Most anything I have learned about the water I have learned from him.

It is evening. The boat seat is as scratchy and dry as a sun-bleached bone. I can feel the faint touch of today's sunshine radiating warm from the splintered wood. It is night now. I have never been out on the creek at night. We have been fishing with hand lines out on the Chester River, our catch is in a basket at my feet, and we are now headed back for the dock.

The boat glides smoothly, the oars digging into the lush deepness of the dark creek. I am straining to recognize this place that is so casually familiar in daylight. The shore is a blur of dark against the night sky—black against navy—as though a painter had blocked it in and will return later to add the details. I can make out the tops of the pines at the marsh edge. They move ever so slightly in the evening breeze and seem taller, menacing, impenetrable.

But I am safe here. I am with Uncle Bill. He knows how to handle everything, especially anything having to do with boats and water. This creek has been his longer than it has been mine. Since childhood he has known it day and night and in all seasons. I am engrossed in finding my way in the dark. He knows where he is going, but I do not want to be merely taken along. I want to know for myself.

I am tired but I would deny it. I am full of sun, rocked by the motion of the boat, ready for home and bed. I listen to the soft slap of the oars. I can sense his muscles tighten as he pulls them through the heavy depths of the creek. They emerge again, arching for their next plunge into the water. I am stunned. The oars are lit—sapphire blue, aqua, green, sparkling, flashing in the dark, plunging downward to the deep again.

"What is that?" I whisper.

"Phosphorous," he answers, as if that explains this marvel.

Again the oars rise dripping blue-green diamonds, their surface alight. *"They light when they're touched,"* he adds.

Another wonder. I forget my navigation and watch as our oars light and sparkle all the way back to the dock.

A few years ago an obituary column in the Centreville paper read something like "Ninety-seven year old native of Baltimore dies here." The woman had moved to Centreville when she was about three months old.[82]

My grandfather called Kent Island the Garden of Eden. Old Mr. Hecker called it "hupa-ma-die country" (translation: hope I may die country, which I assume means that he hoped he could live there until he died). Mr. Hecker referred to anyone he hadn't known for all his life as a "furriner."

Insider, outsider. Which am I? Though I spend most of the year in the city and would be considered a Baltimorean by any measure, I am more at home on this island than in any other place. I am accepted because I am the daughter of a woman who was born and raised here, because Cap'n Eph was a respected man, because Miz Nettie still sits on her porch. I am related.

But beyond that, I am also connected to this land in some way I can't explain. I was dipped in the Chester River before I could walk, before I could speak; a kind of baptism.

I am at the creek by myself today, wading in the shallow water at the edge of the marsh. I walked here from the house, the oyster shell lane blindingly white in the August glare. At the end of the lane I pass our dented mailbox with its crooked red flag and turn at last into the welcome shade of Piney Creek Road.

The road stretches out like an ochre ribbon, its sandy length winding through towering loblolly pines to the edge of the marshy shore. The road is edged with low ditches that sprout fat brown cattails and clumps of deep green reeds. It secretes the rich smell of salt and decaying vegetation.

My cousin, Janeen Clevenger Jewell and I at the Beach Farm, 1946. Note the log I am propped up against as well as the tree stump visible in the background. They are evidence of the steady erosion of Kent Island. Piney Creek also displayed stumps in the shallow water where trees once flourished. Older residents say that changes in the shoreline have been visibly significant in their lifetime. In fact, my grandmother said that she remembered a substantial stand of trees in the spot where this photo was taken. (Author's photo)

Despite my load of dip net, basket, and water jug, I now walk as quickly as possible. The assault of mosquitoes, gnats, and marsh flies is worse in the motionless air and shadow created by the dense pines. These little pests are voracious, biting my legs and buzzing past my ears and eyes with kamikaze abandon. I know that they will attack less frequently when I emerge into the sun and air of the creek.

There is a soft breeze here. The marsh reeds bend and dance in the blinding sun. Dragonflies, all turquoise and green, looking like miniature helicopters, dart about the surface of the creek. The stillness is broken only by the occasional call of a bird or the movement of the breeze through the grass. Though I know that civilization waits back up the sandy road, there is a splendid sense of isolation here.

The afternoon is hot, and although the water is shallow here, it feels refreshingly cool against my bare sunburned legs. The primeval muck pulls at my feet, the mud oozing warm between my toes. The sea grass is thick here; blue crabs hide in seaweed . . . they are the reason I am here.

I crab in the way Uncle Bill taught me, running the flat-edged dip net along the bottom mud, flattening the grass, my eyes alert to movement. When startled, the crabs dash out of hiding, and with a flick of my wrist I must be faster, anticipating their direction and dipping them up. I work with the lead line of the skiff tied around my waist, the little boat following me wherever I go.

A Great Egret, all flashing white with sharp yellow bill appears suddenly amidst the grass. He is startled to see me and we eye each other briefly before he decides that I am not a threat and slowly pokes his way across the marsh on long, slender legs. The marsh is full of animals and birds—egret, heron, hawk, owl, snake, muskrat and raccoon.

There are duck blinds scattered about the marsh. It is here that the hunters will lie in wait for ducks, searching the steel-gray sky for teal, pintail, and canvasback.

"When I was young, the boys were always fishing or hunting. I've eaten all sorts of birds."

"Like different kinds of duck?"

"I'm sure I ate lots of things and didn't know what it was. I remember that they once brought home a swan. You weren't supposed to shoot swan, but they hit one by mistake and so they brought it on home and Mom Mom cooked it."

The blinds, so obvious in the verdant green of summer, will blend into the marsh as the season changes and the grass and bushes turn brown and gold against the bright blue sky.

Then the whistling swan, the Canadian geese, and the numerous species of duck will return to winter on the frosty marsh. No one who has ever heard or seen them can forget the plaintive honking of geese or the thrill of seeing their V formation against a gray and ice-streaked winter sky. Their haunting sounds spark in me some aching of the soul, some ill-defined yearning, some hazily remembered and

The giant soft-shell crab. The photograph is slightly out of focus. (Author's photo)

elusive feeling that is a match for a summer just ended and endless summers lost and irretrievable.

But it is summer still, and long slow days stretch before me. I work through the afternoon, catching a number of hardshell crabs. Under the boat seat, wrapped in seagrass, are three softcrabs—recently molted, their new shells like moist olive satin, and one of them a giant—the largest softcrab I have ever seen.

I took pictures of that crab with my Brownie camera. I posed it on one of Mom Mom's green lawn chairs with a ruler in front of it. It's span from point to point on the top shell was over ten inches and the claws extended over the sides of the generous chair. I'm saving this picture, because when I tell about this crab, people won't believe me!

My father, Marvin Whittle, shows off two large rockfish in 1947. Rockfish were once plentiful. It was not unusual to catch a substantial number with ease, although the good fisherman only took what his family could eat.(Author's photo)

Boats and Fishing and Such

"There is nothing half so much worth doing as messing around in boats."
— *The Wind in the Willows*

The landing at Piney Creek was given to Queen Anne's County by my great-grandfather, Charles Maltimore Nash, during his ownership of the Beach Farm. It was given for the use of local watermen and has been a public landing since that day. The dock at Piney Creek was built by my Uncle Orville and his son, Captain Sonny Nash. A number of skiffs and punts were tied at the dock or to stakes at the shore's edge. The boats were used in a neighborly or communal fashion. If you went to the creek, and required the use of a boat, you simply used one. The understanding was that you did the baling, and the expectation was that you would leave the boat as you found it. If your family boat wasn't there, you could conclude that someone you knew was using it and you could expect its return. Watermen used these boats to row or pole out to their larger craft anchored in the deeper waters of the creek. We also used them for crabbing and fishing within the creek and sometimes for fishing out on the river.

Sunfish, sparkling and iridescent, could be seen swimming about the dock pilings, and we could catch a substantial number without ever leaving the dock.

> The bright little saucer-shaped sunfishes, speckled and brilliantly colored, are a group of beautiful freshwater fishes . . . only a few are common to coastal waters. The pumpkinseed, *lepomis gibbosus*, and the bluegill, *lepomis machrochirus* . . . congregate in shallow protected coves of larger tributaries in summer. . . . They are sparkling, multicolored fishes—blue and green, yellow and orange. They are much alike in appearance, but the pumpkinseed may be identified by the bright orange crescent border on its ear flap and a series of blue and orange stripes

across the lower part of its head. The bluegill has a black earflap and a dark blotch at the base of its dorsal fin. The two species are able to interbreed, so confusing specimens occur.[83]

Catching larger fish necessitated going out on the creek. We fished with bamboo poles, often with spreader hooks, and it was not unusual to catch two fish at a time. The most common fish to catch in the creek was yellow perch (*perca flavescen*).

Yellow perch are freshwater fish so acclimated to the brackish waters that in the Chesapeake Bay region they behave more like semi-anadromous white perch and gizzard shad. They spend most of the year in the upper part of the estuary and return to freshwater in late February and March to spawn in small, shallow streams—Yellow perch are colorful fish, bright yellow to gold with six to eight dark ventrical bands. Spawning males are even more brilliant, with intense orange-red fins.[84]

There were also white perch (*morone americana*), which Lippson describes as a "truly estuarine species" and adds that "each major river system of the Bay apparently maintains its own separate population."[85] Additional abundant species were several varieties of catfish, spot, and croakers. Croakers, called hardheads locally, were frequently fished by hand lines at night. The best of all, of course, was the silver and black-striped rockfish (*morone saxatilis*). Like white perch, the striped bass must spawn upstream in fresh water, the young then migrating toward the Bay.

(White perch and striped bass) are "halfway" anadromous, or semianadromous, as some biologists have labeled them. . . . (they) do not migrate all the way from the ocean, like truly anadromous species, but from the estuarine waters lower down the Bay and rivers. . . . The appearance of small white perch and striped bass a few inches long shows their close family relationship. At this stage, both have longitudinal stripes overlaying a series of vertical bars along their sides.[86]

Rockfish numbers severely declined in the 1970s, but improvements in water quality and strict regulations on catches are allowing the fish to come back in the Chesapeake Bay.

The woods smell of damp and earth and pine. Out in the yard, the sun is warm and bright, and a soft breeze moves lazily through the trees and shrubbery. Here, in the shadow of the pines, the light is dim and muted. The breeze, conquered by the dense and compact branches of the trees, has left the air motionless and still. Sunlight pierces the branches intermittently, lighting the forest floor with occasional patches of gold. It is fairly easy to walk in these woods, because the undergrowth is subdued by a thick carpet of cinnamon-brown needles that have fallen from the high branches of the loblolly pine. It is hushed and quiet here as well, the only sounds an occasional bird call and the crunch of the dry pine carpet under my feet. Sometimes I come to the woods just to wander and explore, to search out the treasures of this place. There are other trees here: oak and sweetgum, maple and sassafras (from whose roots Mom Mom makes a "spring tonic" tea), white pine and cedar, hickory and chestnut, dogwood and holly. There are toadstools, thick banks of velvety green moss, beds of tiny pink ladyslippers—and in one spot and there alone—a bed of waxy Indian pipes.

Today I am gathering pinecones. I have spent many afternoons roaming the soothing stillness of these woods, filling bushel baskets with pinecones and storing them in the barn. They will grow even drier there. Mom Mom will use them as kindling to start her wood stove through the winter.

When autumn brings skies of bright cerulean blue, when all trees but the pine turn yellow, orange, and scarlet, when the first morning frost nips the air, the porch screening will be boarded over and the woodpile and baskets of cones will be moved to the porch.

My mother likes these pinecones, too. She will select the fattest and most symmetrical of them to use as Christmas decorations. In Baltimore at Christmas, we select our tree at a stand a few blocks

The milk house is in the center of the photograph. My grandfather and two other figures stand at the well. Notice the Chesapeake Bay Retriever lounging in the shade (circa 1940). (Author's photo)

from our home. We decorate it with electric lights, multi-colored balls, and strands of silver tinsel. We have a wonderful Christmas garden with a Lionel train that toots and puffs smoke and a little watchman that pops out of the station, swinging his lantern as the train goes by.

"When I was your age," said my mother, "we would chop a cedar tree from the woods and decorate it with old German ornaments and paper chains. We would cut branches of pine and holly to put on the mantle, above the picture frames and over the doors."

"Would you have a Christmas garden, too?"

"Oh, yes. My brothers and I would build it from whatever we had. We would collect things—dried beach sand, shells, rocks, pebbles, pieces of driftwood. We would cut slabs of moss from the woods and use it to build grassy hills. And we had a little white picket fence to go around it. Robert built little things to put in the garden—he built a Matapeake ferry ticket office once. I think Jeannette might still have it."

"Did you have presents?"

"Oh, yes. But not like today. Sometime in early December, Miss Noilly's store would set up a little display of toys and dolls. We would dream about them. Usually we got one toy."

"Just one?"

"Yes, but other things like socks, and a stocking with an orange . . . and walnuts. One Christmas Orville and Jeannette and I walked to Tom Price's store. That's about halfway to Dominion. We wanted to buy Mom Mom a lacquered tray we saw there. We were so proud."

"What else?"

"Well, there was lots of parties and visiting."

"Tell me about that."

"Well, after Christmas Day we would go to visit each other's houses— you know, the twelve days of Christmas. Each night they would decide whose house we were going to the next night. Mom Mom and Miz Lizzie would bake for days ahead of time. They would wrap up their cakes in dishtowels and old newspapers and store them in an old washboiler in the attic. There were sandwiches, potato salad, and lots of cakes and homemade root beer, lemonade, wine, and coffee. And sometimes they would dance. They would push the furniture out of the way, roll up the carpets and wax the floors. There would be music, usually a fiddle or banjo or guitar. Sometimes there was a little band from Queenstown called the Midnight Ramblers."

I really do appreciate the wonders of my Baltimore Christmas garden and our beautifully decorated tree, but I like the Christmas she describes. I am intrigued by this possibility to design, invent, and create Christmas instead of buying it at a store.

My grandmother, like a farmer, follows a well-worn path through a calendar of seasonal activity. There were things to be planted, tended, harvested, preserved. Fruit trees, berry patch, arbor, and garden supplied the food that she would prepare for the winter.

The milk house sits directly across from the porch door, next to the well. It is a small building, both six feet wide and deep and built in a

Germanic style with a high peaked roof of moss-covered slate. The outer walls are of weathered red lap siding, and the planked door, slatted windows, and scalloped trim are an equally weathered shade of blue. A thick block of wood forms a step to the interior where the walls are of thick whitewashed plaster.

"Why do you call it a milk house if it doesn't have any milk in it?"

"Oh, it used to have milk back when we had cows. We would put some of the milk here to let the cream rise to the surface and then we would skim it off to make butter. And I would make clabber and cottage cheese from the skimmed milk."

She opened the latch of the blue planked door. I am carrying a tray of small jars filled with the jelly made from the bounty of the Concord grape arbor. Shelving lines the walls and on them sit neat rows of mason jars filled with summer harvest: green beans, tomatoes, pepper relish, apple butter, ketchup, green tomato pickle, pepper rings, peaches, pears, and plums. Small jars of preserves and jellies sparkle like multicolored jewels in the sunshine from the open door: crabapple, blackberry, damson, peach, quince, and strawberry. It is a room full of loving labor, sealed in paraffin and glass; to taste them is to recapture summer again.

Recipes Served on the Porch

PEPPER RELISH

12 green peppers
12 red peppers
14 large onions

Chop vegetables coarsely. Scald and let stand 5 minutes. Drain, scald again and let stand 10 minutes. Drain and add:

1 quart vinegar	1 oz. celery seed
2 oz. mustard seed	2 tbsp. salt
3 cups sugar	

Cook for 15 minutes after it begins to boil. Seal in mason jars and process in hot water bath.

CATSUP

Boil until well cooked (about 2 hours):

½ bushel ripe tomatoes	6 onions
3 tbsp. allspice	1 tbsp. whole cloves

Strain through a coarse sieve and add:

½ tsp. red pepper	1 oz. black pepper
1 oz. dry mustard	1 lb. brown sugar
1 quart vinegar	½ c. salt

Mix good and boil until thick. Pour into mason jars and process in hot water bath, or pour into glass bottles and cork. When cool, dip tops in melted paraffin wax to seal.

GREEN TOMATO PICKLE

1 peck of green tomatoes
12 onions
4 hot peppers (or 1/3 tsp. red pepper)
4 red sweet peppers
4 green sweet peppers
1 tsp. combined of ground cinnamon, allspice and clove
    (combined in a cloth bag)
2 tbsp. mustard seed
2 tbsp. celery seed
½ gallon vinegar
3 lb. sugar

Chop tomatoes, add a little salt and let stand about one hour. Drain. Grind remainder of ingredients and combine and boil one hour. When nearly finished add:

1 tbsp. tumeric
1 tbsp. dry mustard

Seal in mason jars and process in hot water bath.

STRAWBERRY PRESERVES

Put 3 cups of cleaned and hulled strawberries in a pot. Add nothing else at first; cook slowly for 5 minutes, stirring all the time so they won't scorch. To each 1 cup of strawberries, add 2/3 cup sugar. (This is an approximate measure; the exact recipe states: "I used one of those large cups of mine piled up.") Boil rapidly for 15 minutes. Let cool, pour into glass jars and seal with paraffin wax.

CHILI SAUCE

½ peck ripe tomatoes   3 tbsp. salt
6 green peppers   2 c. vinegar
2 large onions   ½ can mixed spice
1 tbsp. celery seed

Skin tomatoes. Chop tomatoes, onion, and green pepper. Add vinegar, sugar, salt, and celery seed. Cook 1 hour over slow flame, add spices in muslin bag. Continue cooking until well flavored and sauce is thick. Remove bag. Cool and process as in catsup recipe.

They have finished building the new concrete road. It sits about a quarter mile from the porch. On Sunday afternoons, the cars returning from the beach line up to wait their turn to cross the new Bay Bridge. The line backs up as far as I can see and is much longer than any line the little ferries ever had.

We do not go out on Sundays because it is too hard to get back home. Sometimes a car engine will overheat and a stranger will hike across the field to ask for water from the well.

We must become accustomed to new sounds. We can hear the cars and trucks speed by, but we cannot hear the birds as well. More and more trucks go by at night, subduing the familiar songs of the frogs and crickets.

It is evening and the adults are on the porch, sitting around the claw-footed table, playing cards. I am bored with their game and go outside. Only steps from the porch I am in inky darkness, and I turn around to see them, laughing and happy, much loved, sitting in a little pool of yellow light.

The outside world is transformed and unfamiliar at night. I walk about the yard, the grass beneath my feet is soft and already damp with dew. The frogs and crickets have taken up their unvarying evening symphony, seeming to grow louder as I drift across the yard. The only illumination is the lemon-colored moon, and stretching above me in the black sky, a sparkling blanket of stars. At night the spiders spin intricate webs among the shrubbery; at just the right angle the combination of moonlight and dew make them look as though they are strung with diamonds.

I wander back to the porch; I am sleepy but I do not want to climb the steps to bed all alone. I go into the parlor and lie down on the scratchy couch, listening to the pendulum clock tick-tock in unison with the crickets and the frogs.

Last Thanksgiving we had a family dinner in the parlor. Practically the whole family was here, the little house fairly bursting with people, a table the width of the room, the shelf above the wood stove lined with pies, the house enveloped in the smells of roasting turkey, sage and stuffing, sauerkraut and pork.

Uncle Orville and Sonny played their banjos. Aunt Jeannette reached into her memory for the words to old songs and they sang "The Letter Edged in Black" and "The Baggage Coach Ahead."

There is a song that they like but will not sing.

Mom Mom once had a close friend named Maggie who married Pop's brother John. Maggie conceived her first child at the age of forty, and since there were no doctors on the island, Mom Mom urged Uncle John to take his wife to Baltimore when the time for delivery drew near. Uncle John thought she worried unnecessarily, but a heeding of her warning might have saved Maggie's life. She and her baby both died in childbirth, the breech birth far beyond the local midwife's skill. There is a song that reminds her of her lost friend, and after all these years, it still brings tears to her eyes.

> *I wander'd today to the hill, Maggie*
> *To watch the scene below;*
> *The creek and the creaking old mill, Maggie*
> *As we used to long ago.*

The green grove is gone from the hill, Maggie
Where first the daisies sprung;
The creaking old mill is still, Maggie
Since you and I were young.

Chorus:
And now we are aged and gray, Maggie
And the trials of life nearly done;
Let us sing of the days that are gone, Maggie
When you and I were young.

A city so silent and lone, Maggie
Where the young and the gay and the best,
In polished white mansions of stone, Maggie
Have found a place of rest.
And join in the songs that were sung
For we sang just as gay as they, Maggie
When you and I were young.

They say I am feeble with age, Maggie
My steps less sprightly than then;
My face is a well-written page, Maggie
But time alone was the pen.
They say we are aged and gray, Maggie
As spray by the white breakers flung;
But to me you're as fair as you were, Maggie
When you and I were young.

I remember that Thanksgiving well. It is not often that we are all together. It runs in my memory like a motion picture . . . the faces, the smiles, the stories from the past; good food and music, silliness and laughter, warmth and love . . . a family bond forged by Johanetta whom we all love.

The adults are still playing cards. I snuggle into the pillows of the couch, the pendulum clock tick-tocking me to sleep.

The years have passed. The world has changed.

Mom Mom died on January 23, 1976, seven months short of her ninety-seventh birthday. Uncle Ed died in 1974, going before her just like the gypsy fortune-teller said.

Uncle Robert is gone, and Uncle Bill, Aunt Lollie, Uncle William, Uncle Orville, and Sonny also gone.

The curio cabinet from the parlor sits in my entry hall, the pendulum clock ticks its same sound from the wall of my kitchen.

Someone broke into the empty house before she died, stripping it of everything except the few things that she had already given away, taking her framed birth certificate, the furniture, the wooden caddy for silverware that my grandfather had made.

Someone else broke in a short time later, perhaps looking for a place to spend the night. They tried to start a fire in one of the closed fireplaces, setting the house ablaze. It was unsalvageable, and the Queen Anne's County fire department had to finish the job, burning it to the ground. We never told her.

Aunt Lil's old tavern was refurbished as a real estate office. The mulberry tree is still there, older, wider, and some of the other trees and shrubs struggle on in the growing wilderness of the farm.

The State of Maryland built that second bridge.

Despite numerous town meetings and protests from residents, they came once again with their trucks and changed the road, altering highway access for many residents. They broke promises about the design, causing many people who have lived on the island all their lives to drive miles in the wrong direction to access this mighty new road. My mother wrote to the governor and he forwarded her letter to the same engineers the landowners had been arguing with in the first place.

The old graveyard still sits isolated and abandoned across their concrete sea. Farms we passed traveling from the ferry are now stretches of lookalike housing, and people with money moor fancy boats and build shopping centers, marinas, and restaurants. I hardly recognize the creek; silted and littered, it is either undiscovered or unwanted by developers.

But the screech of a gull can transport me, the smell of a salt marsh, the memory of faces held dear. I have traveled many places, done many things. With grown children of my own, I am full of the world . . . but my heart still aches for that island that once was Eden.

SAYINGS, TIDBITS and FRAGMENTS

If the truth be known (if we knew what was really true about that)

I don't rightly know (I have an idea, but I don't know for sure)

Carry you off (take you there, drive you there, as in "If you want to go shopping, I'd be happy to carry you off to Centreville.")

Studying and studying (I've been thinking about it, but I'm not certain yet)

I know it so (I know that what you are saying is true)

Gone to the bad (spoiled, rotten)

Dealing (shopping, buying, as in "They always drove to Denton to do their dealing")

Would not let you take care of a chicken laying an egg (You're not responsible enough to take care of something that basically takes care of itself)

A dog that will bring a bone will carry one (a gossip that will tell you a story will tell a story about you)

Idle hands are the devil's workshop (if you're not busy at work, you are going to get into trouble)

The squeaking wheel gets the oil (if you continue to complain, someone will eventually listen to you)

He'd buy a pig in a poke (he is not a good judge of value; a good talker could sell him anything)

They gave him over for dead (He was so hopelessly sick or hurt that they were sure he would die)

I'd allow as how (as in "I'd allow as how he'd do that," meaning, I know that he is that way and probably would behave in that manner)

I rec'lect that (I remember)

If a man starves to death on Kent Island, he is either stupid or lazy or both (if you are a waterman and/or a farmer/gardener, you will always have food)

The Ford is my vehicle
I shall not walk
It costs more than shoe leather
It makes me labor and sweat

Yea, though I ride through the valley
I am towed up hills
If this thing follows me the rest of my life
I'll dwell in the poor house forever.

Red sky at night, sailor's delight;
Red sky at morning, sailors take warning

If your ears burn, someone is talking about you.

If your nose itches, you're going to have company.

If you eat the last piece of food on a plate, you will be an old
    maid.

Hang a horseshoe for good luck; hang it with the ends
    pointed up so that the luck does not run out.

If a job is once begun
Never leave it till it's done
Be the labor great or small
Do it well or not at all

You'll have the best luck soft-crabbing on a full moon and in
    the morning.

A new broom sweeps clean.

Home is where the heart is.

Afterword

Residents of Kent Island, old and new alike, have learned to coexist with the redesigned Route 50. The highway, a major north-south route, is busy year round—but in summer, particularly on weekends, the traffic swells substantially as people strive to "reach the beach." For locals, the travel involved in the activities of normal lives (shopping for groceries, going to the drugstore, to church services, to visit family and friends) is obstructed by the weekend glut of traffic. "If I want to go somewhere on the weekend, I either get there by the back roads or I stay home" confided one resigned resident.

Development continues. The price of real estate steadily escalates, and many "waterfront" or "water view" homes advertised in the *Bay Times* range from significant six-figure price tags to $2 million or more. As the old saw states, God's not making more waterfront property—and everyone wants to live here. As is typical of human nature, the last person to discover this still lovely place is frequently the one who wants to stop the fifty-year migration.

In 2001, residents formed the Kent Island Defense League in opposition to a proposed development by K. Hovnanian Companies, that would include 1,505 homes, an eighty-eight-bed assisted living facility, a 95,000-square-foot shopping center, 216 condominiums, and three hundred rental apartments. The Defense League placed ads in the *Bay Times* urging county commissioners to stop development and resolve such problems as failing septic systems, intense traffic and congestion, and strained volunteer emergency services, and to address issues such as responsible growth management. As one ad read: "Let our County commissioners know you want to preserve our coveted way of life for future generations." Wal-Mart has tangled with both the county commissioners and Kent Island residents over a proposed superstore near the bridge. At present both disputes are unresolved, and additional projects loom on the horizon. Currently a moratorium, or building permit cap, is in place in Queen Anne's County, the stated purpose of which is to "provide the county with the opportunity to prepare and adopt the necessary tools to address future growth."[87]

Others would accurately point out that development has brought economic growth, business opportunity, improved shopping, and increased services and conveniences to the island—things that might never have appeared without the bridge(s), highway, and increased population.

Stevensville remains charming, with well-maintained turn-of-the-century houses and interesting shops, restaurants, and artist's studios. From the highway, Chester is difficult to distinguish within the blur of commercial development.

The Kent Island Heritage Society, whose membership ranges from old-timers to recent residents, is committed to documenting the rich history of the island. In addition to maintaining historical files, the society has restored, or are in the process of restoring, the Cray House, the old Stevensville train depot, and the Kirwan House. Each spring, the society sponsors *Kent Island Days*, a festival commemorating the founding of the Kent Island colony.

The Cross Island Trail, recently completed, extends for five miles from Terrapin Park near Stevensville to the new Chesapeake Exploration Center at Kent Narrows. The trail edges both shoreline and roadway, and passes through stretches of marsh, pinewood, and farmland. There are places along the trail when the highway traffic is out of earshot, where the view is unobstructed—places where you might imagine yourself on a Kent Island of a much earlier time. A section of the trail turns down Piney Road, past the entrance to the Beach Farm, cutting through the woods at the edge of what was my grandmother's farm before crossing the creek to Kent Narrows. It is a new trail over land steeped in history, a trail for walkers, inline skaters and cyclists that stretches over earth once traversed by the Indians, seventeenth-century Englishmen, farm families, and oystermen who once called Kent Island home.

Notes

[1] George L. Davis, *The Day Star of American Freedom, or the Birth and Early Growth of Toleration in the Province of Maryland* (Baltimore, 1855), 110.

[2] "Land Notes 1634–1655," *Maryland Historical Magazine,* 6 (1911): 60–61.

[3] Hamill Kenny, *The Origin and Meaning of the Indian Place Names of Maryland* (Baltimore: Waverly Press, 1961), 87–88.

[4] *Travels and Works of Captain John Smith,* edited by Edward Arber, with critical introduction by A. G. Bradley (Edinburgh: John Grant, 1910), 349–50.

[5] George Alsop, *A Character of the Province of Maryland* (London, 1666), 72–73.

[6] Emily Roe Denny, *Indians of Kent Island* (1960), 5. Mrs. Denny spent many years teaching English at Stevensville High School and is a teacher my mother remembers with great fondness.

[7] These forms of food gathering and maintenance are extensively discussed in Helen C. Rountree and Thomas E. Davidson, *Eastern Shore Indians of Virginia and Maryland* (Charlottesville: University Press of Virginia, 1997).

[8] Robert J. Brugger, *Maryland: A Middle Temperament, 1634–1980* (Baltimore: Johns Hopkins University Press, 1988), 33.

[9] Bernard C. Steiner, *Beginnings of Maryland, 1631–1639* (Baltimore: Johns Hopkins University Press, 1903), 363.

[10] J. Thomas Scharf, *History of Maryland from the Earliest Period to the Present Day.* 3 vols. (1879; repr., Hatboro, Pa.: Tradition Press, 1967), 136.

[11] Ibid., 138.

[12] Denny, *Indians of Kent Island,* 5.

[13] Margaret C. Schoch, *Of History and Houses: A Kent Island Heritage* (Queenstown, Md.: The Queen Anne Press, 1982), 48.

[14] Scharf, *History of Maryland,* 138.

[15] Ibid., 138.

[16] Reginald V. Truitt, *Kent Island: Maryland's Oldest Settlement* (Stevensville, Md.: Women of Christ Church, 1965), 5.

[17] Frederic Emory, *Queen Anne's County, Maryland: Its Early History and Development* (Baltimore: Maryland Historical Society, 1950), 64.

[18] "Correspondence of Governor Sharpe," *Maryland Historical Magazine,* 12 (1917): 370–71.

[19] Emory, *Queen Anne's County,* 65.

[20] "Ring Bells! Beat Gongs! Here Comes the Smokey Joe," Kent Island Heritage Society files, 1938.

[21] Ibid.

[22] Brugger, *Middle Temperament,* 577.

[23] J. E. Greiner, Consulting Engineers, *The Chesapeake Bay Bridge Engineering Report* (Baltimore, 1948), 48.

[24] Statistics obtained from Ron Smith, Maryland Department of Transportation, telephone interview with the author, February 23, 1999.

[25] *Kent Island Bay Times,* September 28, 1998, 1.

[26] Truitt, *Kent Island,* 7.

[27] Denny, *Indians of Kent Island,* 4.

[28] Truitt, *Kent Island,* 4.

[29] *Where River and Bay Waves Meet* (Kent Island, Md.: The Love Point Beach and Park Company, Inc., n.d.).

[30] Pat Emory, "Love Point Culled from Kemp," *Kent Island Bay Times,* September 28, 1972, 6; L. L. Hubble, "I Remember Vacation Pleasures at the Old Love Point Hotel," *Baltimore Sun Magazine,* May 12, 1968.

[31] Mary K. Tilghman, "Hotel Love Point," *Kent Island Bay Times,* November 3, 1982.

[32] Hotel Love Point and Beach advertisement, Kent Island Heritage Society.

[33] "Old Hotel Destroyed in a Flaming Frenzy," *Kent Island Bay Times,* November 19, 1965.

[34] *Kent Island Bay Times,* April 9, 1970.

[35] *History of the Schools of Kent Island Queen Anne's County Maryland* (Queen Anne's County, Md.: Kent Island Heritage Society), 20.

[36] Ibid., 22.

[37] Billy Harris, a lifelong Kent Island waterman and the owner of Harris's Crab House at Kent Narrows, is also the grandson of John and Enola Taylor, proprietors of the general store discussed on pp. 75–77.

[38] Erich Isaac, "The First Century of the Settlement of Kent Island" (Ph.D. diss., Johns Hopkins University, 1957), 216.

[39] Emory, *Queen Anne's County,* 23.

[40] Ibid., 24.

[41] Isaac, "First Century of the Settlement of Kent Island," 216.

[42] Emory, *Queen Anne's County, Maryland,* 8.

[43] John R. Wennersten, *The Oyster Wars of Chesapeake Bay* (Centreville, Md.: Tidewater Publishers, 1981), 7.

[44] A. J. Nichols, *The Oyster Packing Industry of Baltimore* (Baltimore:

University of Maryland, 1937), 4.

[45] The origin of this term is explained by Paula Johnson in *Working the Water: The Commercial Fisheries of Maryland's Patuxent River* (Charlottesville: University Press of Virginia, 1988). Johnson states that the term "cove oysters"—which appears on labels and in advertising of the day—was a reference to Baltimore's Cove Street, where many of the oyster packers and canners operated.

[46] Frederic J. Parks, *The Celebrated Oysterhouse Cookbook* (Allentown, Pa.: Park's Seafood, 1985), 6.

[47] Truitt, *Kent Island*, 9.

[48] *Genealogy and Biography of Leading Families of the City of Baltimore and Baltimore County, Maryland* (New York: Chapman Publishing Co, 1897), 807.

[49] Ibid., 808.

[50] Johnson, *Working the Water*, 41.

[51] Ann Wilmer, "Floating Theatre Brought Drama, Laughter to Shore," *The Shoreman*, 22: No. 8, 84.

[52] Ibid., 85.

[53] Robert H. Burgess, *This Was Chesapeake Bay* (Cambridge, Md.: Cornell Maritime Press, 1963).

[54] Wilmer, "Floating Theatre," 85.

[55] Jacques Kelly, "Novel, Operetta Help Recall Memory of Floating Theatre," *Baltimore Sun*, October 3, 1988.

[56] *Newsletter of the Kent Island Heritage Society*, December 1986, 84.

[57] Ibid., June 1986, 68.

[58] *Queenstown News*, July 31, 1953.

[59] Ibid.

[60] Ibid.

[61] Paul Wilstach, *Tidewater Maryland* (Centreville, Md.: Tidewater Publishers, 1969), 52.

[62] Emory, *Queen Anne's County*, 283, 287, 290.

[63] Wennersten, *Oyster Wars*, 9.

[64] Emory, *Queen Anne's County*, 493.

[65] *Newsletter of the Kent Island Heritage Society*, September 1985, 43.

[66] *Centreville Observer*, July 11, 1917.

[67] Ibid.

[68] John C. Hayman, *Rails Along the Chesapeake: A History of Railroading on the Delmarva Penninsula, 1827–1978* (n.p.: Marvadel Publishers, 1979), 123.

[69] *Newsletter of the Kent Island Heritage Society*, June 1985, 39.

[70] Ibid., Spring 1982, 13.

[71] The carvings of Captain Orville Nash and his son, Captain Sonny Nash, are discussed by Hugo Gemignani in *The Forgotten Seven: The Decoy Carvers of Kent Island* (Stevensville, Md.: The Author, 1992).

[72] Emory, *Queen Anne's County*, 44.

[73] Ibid.; *Newsletter of the Kent Island Heritage Society*, June 1985, 40.

[74] "$48 Million Span over Kent Narrows to Ease Traffic Snarls," *Baltimore Sunday Sun*, November 15, 1987, 14E.

[75] Clarence Gould, *Christ Church Parish* (Stevensville, Md.: Kent Island Heritage Society, 1959), 21.

[76] Emory, *Queen Anne's County*, 143; Gould, *Christ Church Parish*, 22.

[77] Emory, *Queen Anne's County*, 144.

[78] Ibid., 145.

[79] Ibid., 146.

[80] *The 1877 Atlases and Other Early Maps of the Eastern Shore of Maryland* (Wicomico County, Md.: Wicomico Bicentennial Commission, 1976), 134–35.

[81] *Gazette for Maryland & District of Columbia*, 1871, 684–85.

[82] Boyd Gibbons, *Wye Island* (Baltimore: Johns Hopkins University Press, 1977), 75.

[83] Alice Jane Lippson and Robert L. Lippson, *Life in the Chesapeake Bay*, 2d ed. (Baltimore: Johns Hopkins University Press, 1997), 130.

[84] Ibid., 128.

[85] Ibid., 120.

[86] Ibid., 121.

[87] *Kent Island Bay Times*, July 24, 2002.